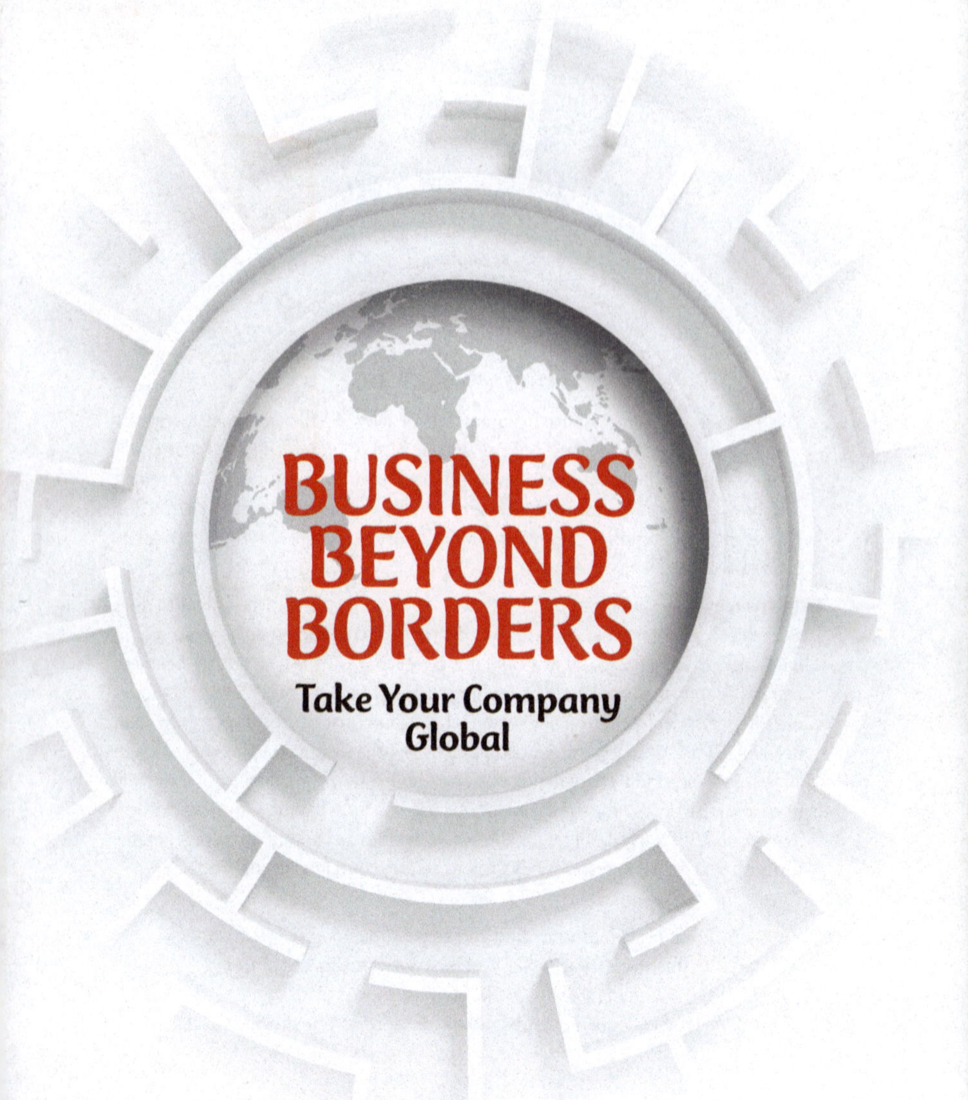

BUSINESS BEYOND BORDERS

Take Your Company Global

CYNTHIA DEARIN

The material in this publication is of the nature of general comment only, and does not represent professional advice. It is not intended to provide specific guidance for particular circumstances and it should not be relied on as the basis for any decision to take action or not take action on any matter which it covers. Readers should obtain professional advice on any matter where appropriate, before making any such decision. To the maximum extent permitted by law, the author and publisher disclaim all responsibility and liability to any person or company, arising directly or indirectly from any person or company taking or not taking action based on the information in this publication. While all reasonable attempt at factual accuracy has been made, the author accepts no responsibility for any errors contained in this book.

Book design, composition and artwork by Robyn Greathead,
Treehouse Type & Art Workers. www.treehouse.com.au
Edited by Damian Clarke. www.suppleminds.org
Proof-reading by Fiona Regan. www.linkedin.com/in/fiona-regan-4b3296101

ISBN: 978-0-9942442-2-2

NATIONAL LIBRARY OF AUSTRALIA
A catalogue record for this work is available from the National Library of Australia

"If you are a global player or planning to become one, Business Beyond Borders provides valuable guidance and insights on how to successfully turn your export strategy into a winning one. Full of examples and case studies, this book is a 'must have' to learn from business owners who have actually made it. A real tool to help you translate your strategy into an action plan!"

Tatiana Miron
Founder of Prime Target

"If I reflect on the veritable ocean of books, videos and blogs attempting to explain how to enter and prosper in global markets, most are incomplete. This is because generally, there is no adequate framework of thinking that recognises the dual (contradictory!) influences on growth: change and stability. Many authors deal with the change element in an appealing way, identify the dynamism and opportunities of chasing down clients and servicing new markets. But this is the middle step. On either side is firstly the establishment and finally survival of the business, both of which rely on and revert to basic stability, particularly in business knowledge and management techniques. Cynthia has brought us a book that instructs on both the dynamic aspects and challenges of foreign trade, while integrating and explaining the array of bedrock skills that build and maintain a strong international business. As such, we now have a very practical guide for start-ups and established traders. Buy it."

Bill Cole
Partner, BDO Australia

Acknowledgements

While the author is responsible for the writing, no book comes to life without the wisdom, guidance and support of many people. *Business Beyond Borders* is no exception.

Since I began work on the concept for the book in 2017, I have conducted interviews and had numerous conversations with business owners and experts from around the world. In particular, I would like to thank Gary Garner, Thomas Vo, Alan Oppenheim, Alicia Navarro, Peter Evans, Michael Barron, Vanessa Garrard, Tom Griffith, Dai Williams, Jane Jackson, Simon Kaiyu Li, Stacey Ellis Fisher and Lorraine Cherry-Nguyen, Clive White, Peter Geoghegan, Penny Crawford, Lara Tarakjian, Zach Person, Jackie Barnes, Steve Plakotaris, Barry Wafer and Zach Selch, for the time they spent sharing their ideas and experiences with me. The anecdotes and gems of insight gleaned from these interactions have stayed with me and are scattered throughout the chapters.

My manuscript would never have become a book without my editing and design team. Thanks to Damian Clarke for improving the copy and persevering with the project through your own international move, with a family, in the middle of a pandemic. To Robyn Greathead, your amazing design sensibility and attention to detail never ceases to blow me away. Thank you for your immense care and effort to ensure that *Business Beyond Borders* is as perfect as it can be. And to Fiona Regan, I'm grateful for your input on proof-reading – your eagle eye was indispensable to ensuring that the text was flawless.

The Dearin & Associates team deserves a special vote of thanks, for pressing me to complete the book and for supporting me to get it into the world. Your encouragement and support has meant a lot and I am very grateful for all your hard work on this project.

And lastly, to my husband, Pete. Thank you for believing in me, for supporting me, for caring for our children and cooking me countless meals while I wrote and rewrote the manuscript. Words cannot express how grateful I am.

CONTENTS

INTRODUCTION

In 1989 my parents took me overseas for the first time. We travelled from Sydney, Australia to Singapore, to Tashkent and on to Moscow for a week, before finally arriving in London, where we spent several months.

Those were extraordinary times – the Berlin wall was coming down, communism was ending and globalisation was starting to surge. As an impressionable twelve year old, that journey had a big impact on me and was a defining influence on how I chose to shape my life. I had always been interested in other countries and I loved helping people. I decided that I wanted to be a diplomat.

Fast forward 15 years and you will find me sitting in a corner office in an embassy, gazing out over the desert, disillusioned. I had achieved my dream, been accepted into the Department of Foreign Affairs and Trade as a graduate, trained as an Arabist and been sent to represent Australia in the Middle East. It was a huge honour, and I should have been ecstatic, but I was not. Despite all the glamour, I could not see the point of a lot of what I did. Even though I was working with Australian citizens and companies, I did not seem to be creating a real difference for people, which was what I had always aimed to do.

A couple of years later, to the astonishment of almost everyone I knew, I gave up the dream job and went to London for postgraduate study. Armed with some more qualifications, I became a management consultant and spent four years in Iraq, working with the British and US governments to get the country back on its feet. That was an intense period of my life. Amazing work, real impacts, but also lots of danger. Extraordinary as it was, it could not last forever, and when the political will to see Iraq transformed evaporated, my role went with it.

I came home to Australia and took a job running an industry association that represented Australian businesses internationally. After a couple of years, I ran into the same problem I had faced as a diplomat – I was deeply unsatisfied because I could not see how my work created real value for people.

And so, in fear and trembling, I quit my job and started out on my own. It was just me, my kitchen table and a blank sheet of paper. It was scary. I knew that I wanted to help companies to scale internationally. I had loads of exotic professional expertise, but limited understanding of how to create something powerful, something valuable that would change lives by helping companies to get incredible products and services into the hands of people across the world.

That is the journey I have been on since 2013 and this book is the result of what I have learned along the way. It is about how to create a successful strategy for scaling internationally, so that you can multiply your impact on the world by a factor of ten.

Many business leaders dream of expanding their company's footprint into international markets, but the majority never get there.

I have been working internationally for 22 years and of the hundreds of business leaders I have come across, only a handful have what it takes to be an international success – a crystal clear vision, a powerful plan and the momentum and resources to make the dream a reality.

The majority of businesses expand globally by launching a series of half thought-out concepts and steer the ship on 'gut feel'. Often it does not end well.

Although the challenges are many, I believe there has never been a better time to go global. Because of the way in which technology has shrunk the world, 99.9% of the people you could serve are no longer in your hometown, your home state or even your country. These days, you can reach customers in ways that were impossible just a few years ago and you can get your message and your products out to millions of people.

In this book, I set out to show you the steps to creating a successful international business and how to avoid the mistakes that bring you undone.

I hope it serves you well.

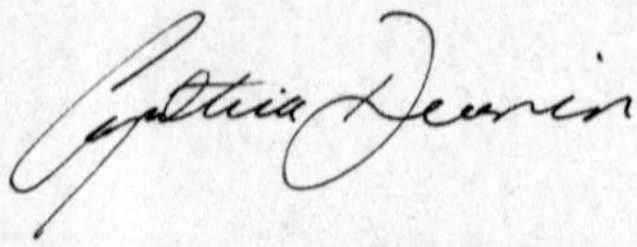

CHAPTER 1 WHY YOU NEED AN INTERNATIONAL STRATEGY – EVEN NOW!

CHAPTER 1

WHY YOU NEED AN INTERNATIONAL STRATEGY – EVEN NOW!

As this book goes to press, the COVID-19 pandemic is reshaping the global business landscape and the world as we know it. For many executives, just surviving is a fight to the death and expanding internationally is the last thing on their minds.

But if you are a business leader with big dreams, you still need an international strategy. COVID-19 has slowed the movement of goods and all-but-halted the movement of people, but global business is not going away. It is evolving. To keep up, grow, and flourish, you need to evolve too.

The death of distance is a key driver for international business, even as we grapple with COVID-19. Massively improved supply chain logistics, travel and technology are enabling goods, people and ideas to move around the world faster than at any other time in history.

Activities that previously had to be done in one place have been unbundled and spread out around multiple geographies. In many industries, especially elaborately transformed manufactures[1], supply chains have become truly global. New technologies let us meet people on the other side of the world, transmit our data across the globe in a heartbeat and make and receive payments in the space of a few minutes. Services including telemedicine, architecture, design, accounting, coaching, management consulting, and dozens of others can be provided from virtually anywhere, irrespective of where the customer is.

The death of distance has implications for almost everyone in business because we can communicate and work with customers and suppliers who were unreachable just a few short years ago. For now, global trade in goods has slowed, but it will eventually return to historic levels because the movement of goods is far less risky than the movement of people. That said, I believe that we will see a big, permanent step change in the way services are sold.

The increase in technology-driven service delivery that we have seen in the last decade is just the tip of the iceberg. As COVID-19 forces people out of public spaces and prevents us from gathering, the landscape is changing rapidly. Those of us who preferred face-to-face meetings and baulked at virtual business coaching, management consulting, legal advice and medical support, are coming to terms with the fact that, for now, this is how it is. Like it or not, telehealth and Zoom socials are a reality and, for many people, almost the only contact that they have with others. As populations get more comfortable with the new normal, I predict that we will see a rapid acceleration of the technology trends that were already taking off before the virus took hold, and a bunch of new ones too.

Limitless opportunity means unbridled competition

For services providers, this means international markets will be more accessible than ever before. Increased uptake of technology-enabled service delivery equals lower barriers to entry. In other words, if you have a great product that can be delivered without you needing to be there in person, and a powerful message that resonates with your audience, you suddenly have almost limitless potential to sell anywhere.

The downside to limitless opportunity is a massive increase in competition. If barriers to entry fall and you can suddenly sell anywhere, people from all over the world can suddenly sell into your home market too. And if they can create and sell a better product at less cost and market it with equal flair, that is the end of your market share. The truth is that the dark side of borderless markets – increased competition – should be just as great a driver for a perceptive CEO as its bright side – increased opportunity.

Even if you put current global trends aside, the classic reasons for international scale continue to matter.

Reach more customers

Access to international markets enables access to more customers. This matters for any company that only has clients in one geography, and is especially true if you are based in a country that has a relatively small domestic market.

Over the last 20 years the global marketplace has grown by 3 to 4 billion new customers, to a total of around 7.6 billion people. This reflects the way in which economies have evolved in that time. Not so long ago, China and India were still considered developing countries. These days, they are leading economies whose rapidly expanding middle classes have money to spend. Similar trends are apparent elsewhere in the world as the middle classes grow rapidly throughout Asia, the Middle East and Latin America. In many cases, 99% of the people you could sell to are now located outside your own country.

According to the Brookings Institute, the next decade could see an even faster expansion of the middle class than at any other time in history. Globally, the middle class is already spending $35 trillion annually, and could be spending $64 trillion by 2030, accounting for roughly a third of projected GDP growth. Within a few years, based on current forecasts, most of the world's population could have middle-class or rich lifestyles for the first time ever.

This explosion of middle-class populations with increased purchasing power and a hunger for higher standards of living has generated huge demand for all types of products and services, which host countries often cannot meet. The sheer volume of the opportunity that the rising middle class represents can be difficult to grasp. For example:

India's electronics market, valued at USD 120 billion in FY17/18, is expected to grow to USD 400 billion by 2025.[2]

And in China, high quality Australian milk can sell for up to $9 per litre, compared to its $1.50 to $4 price tag in Australia.

Incredibly, even these enormous markets for 'traditional' products are dwarfed by the opportunities in emerging sectors. For instance, the global market size of Internet of Things (IoT) platforms was USD 1,340 million in 2017 and is expected to reach USD 9,960 million by the end of 2025[3]. And these examples are not outliers. Do a quick Google search for your sector – you will find dozens of opportunities of the same magnitude.

Many multinationals, tech giants and luxury brands have gone on the front foot to gain a first mover advantage and position themselves to capture middle class consumers as they move out of poverty and into the middle income bracket. The good news is that micro-to-medium-sized businesses can capitalise on these opportunities too. Plenty of smaller companies are carving out their niche in international markets and gaining access to new clients that they would not have won had they stayed at home.

CASE STUDY: Siteminder

Mike Ford and Mike Rogers started Siteminder in 2006. It began as a two-person operation working out of a rental home on Sydney's northern beaches. The company now has more than 800 staff, services over 35,000 hotels around the world and generates more than AU$100 million in annual recurring revenue. Eighty per cent of Siteminder's turnover comes from offshore. It processes 87 million hotel reservations a year, or $38 billion worth of hotel, Airbnb or bed and breakfast stays. These days, Siteminder is considered one of the 20 greatest pioneering technology companies to come out of Australia and New Zealand.

CASE STUDY: Emma and Tom's

Australian juice and snack company Emma and Tom's was founded in 2004 by childhood friends Emma Welsh and Tom Griffith. Getting a fruit-based drinks business off the ground was anything but easy in the early years. The first batches did not taste good, Emma and Tom could not get anyone to manufacture their instantly recognisable bottles, and the distribution just was not working.

Today, Emma and Tom's is an international brand, sold in Jordan, Dubai, Hong Kong, Singapore and Malaysia.

CASE STUDY: Jane Jackson, Career Management Coach

Jane Jackson is a career management coach and solopreneur who services clients all around the world. Originally from Hong Kong, Jane established her coaching business in Australia in 2001 and recognised the opportunity that rapid advancements in technology offered her business.

Instead of flying around the world to deliver training for her clients, Jane began using videoconference technology while maintaining the same standards of service as her in-person clients received. She discovered that changing her delivery model radically changed her business as well. Jane was able to reach hundreds of new clients while dramatically reducing the cost of providing advice. She saved time, money and energy by working remotely, and maintained a healthy profit margin. Today, Jane has worked with over 8,000 professionals from Asia and Australia to reinvigorate their careers.

CASE STUDY: Skimlinks

Alicia Navarro founded her automated affiliate marketing firm, Skimlinks, in Australia in 2012. When she realised that there was virtually no market for her product in Australia, Alicia moved her operation to the United Kingdom. Through her clients in London, she was able to target many of their parent companies in the United States as well. Two years later, the company expanded to the US market. Today, Skimlinks facilitates $1 billion worth of transactions for its clients and is used by more than 4 million websites worldwide.

Spread your risks

The expression 'don't put all your eggs in one basket' applies equally to investment portfolios and customer bases. In an investment context, you spread risk among different types of assets to protect the portfolio against wild price fluctuations. The same principle applies to a company's customer base. A business can pay dearly if too many of its customers are concentrated in one country and conditions change quickly. If you only sell in one market and there is a downturn, new competitors appear, regulations change or your machinery fails – damaging your product and losing you a major contract – sales may drop dramatically, putting the company at serious risk.

Diversifying your markets offsets risk in the domestic market by opening-up opportunities with new clients, new partnerships and joint ventures, as well as new opportunities to develop products for specific geographies. Diversification can also help smaller companies survive tough economic times and political volatility – factors which are increasingly important as global politics and the dynamics of international trade continue to shift rapidly and unpredictably.

Companies that operate in several markets typically have a more sustainable business, with better sales growth and higher margins. And if you are a small company that wants to get into a large company's supply chain, being in different markets is particularly useful because you can tell the bigger players that you have experience in these markets. That gives you a leg up when approaching large global firms and buyers.

Protect against competitors

International expansion does not just let you reach more customers. It is also a hedge against the competition and it has never been more important than now. As I mentioned above, the transformation of global economies has created 3 to 4 billion newly minted consumers. It has also created a sea of well-educated, hard-working people with aspirations – meet your new competitors.

In the services sector, it's becoming easier and easier for these competitors to take your clients as technology continues to shrink the world. You do not need a big imagination to see how a surge of new, international competitors could threaten your market share.

When it comes to goods, tariffs were once a major hurdle to doing business internationally, and a barrier to competition. That is generally not the case anymore, despite the US-China trade war that has plagued international markets recently. Sixty years of trade liberalisation has dramatically reduced tariffs, making it cheaper to sell goods overseas and compete with locally produced products. In some senses, this is a plus. But low tariffs also make it easier for international competitors to sell into your domestic market. Sooner or later, most sectors will face threats from foreign entrants, and in sectors like retail, local players are already feeling the squeeze.

Foreign competitors are not the only worry. Even if you are confident that your industry is safe from external threats, you cannot afford to ignore the threats at home. Some of your canny domestic competitors have already realised that they can turn geo-arbitrage to their favour. They are using web developers and designers from Jamaica, graphic designers from Hungary and Slovenia, bookkeepers from India and virtual assistants from the Philippines to source services for themselves and their clients at a fraction of the cost of buying domestically. And that means they can reduce their cost of goods sold and undercut you, while still making a profit. I work with companies that have built their entire offering around the geo-arbitrage model, and they are doing well.

Expanding overseas remains a smart way to counter the threat from overseas competitors and from local firms capitalising on geo-arbitrage to compete with you at home.

Control costs

Every astute CEO wants to reduce expenses and entering the global arena can help to achieve this.

Across Asia, countries are competing to attract foreign businesses to set-up onshore, by offering low taxes and setup costs for companies. Vietnam and Malaysia are leaders in this space and both markets also offer extremely high-speed internet and attractive living conditions, making them emerging hubs for the media sector.

If done correctly, using offshore resources can be a highly effective way to reduce costs. In Asia and India top talent is available across a range of business functions at a fraction of the cost of hiring the same person at home. This trend is no longer just the domain of big organisations. Growing numbers of smaller companies now rely heavily on virtual assistants and back-office staff, as well as professionals including programmers, engineers, architects and accountants from countries with lower costs of living and employment.

You may also find more economical solutions to your production and manufacturing challenges offshore. However, COVID-19 has manufacturers everywhere re-evaluating their supply chain reliability and looking for supply chain solutions closer to home.

Maximise profits

Overseas markets may generate higher returns for your business, especially if they are less advanced, attractive or competitive than your domestic market, or harder to do business in. Difficult markets usually attract fewer foreign companies. You may find a blank space in the market that you can fill, potentially allowing you to charge a higher premium than you can attract at home. Niche milk-producing companies, Bellamy's Organic and The a2 Milk Company – which sell infant formula products to China at higher retail prices than they can command at home – are good examples of companies that have tapped international markets to maximise profits.

Expansion equals innovation

In an era when robots are replacing highly trained professionals, business leaders cannot afford to be complacent about innovation. The commercial and technological environment is changing so quickly that those who stand still will be left behind.

The good news is that research suggests that operating internationally drives innovation[4]. In other words, if you want a company that is more innovative, productive and competitive, look offshore. Exposure to new ideas and clients, and the challenge of generating solutions to new problems, will help you and your team become more innovative and more productive, creating an enduring competitive edge, at home and abroad. The result? A virtuous circle with the potential to drive further international success.

The word 'innovation' conjures up images of ground-breaking new inventions and revolutionary technologies, but most innovations are an evolution, rather than a revolution. A change to your processes, delivery model or even your marketing can be just as effective as a new product in creating a lasting competitive advantage, increasing margins and helping you unlock profitable new markets.

Here are five different ways that small companies can use innovation in international markets to drive growth:

- **Product and service innovation.** Selling internationally can help you find a broader customer base for an innovative, niche product that may have a limited market onshore. It also lets you capitalise on innovative product features with unique appeal offshore – the same features which might not appeal at home.

  Sean Ashby's aussieBum apparel brand is a living case study of product innovation on the international stage. After his concept was scorned in his native Australia, Ashby took his ideas overseas, securing none other than luxury London department store Selfridges as his first stockist. These days, aussieBum has global sales of more than $150 million.[5]

On the flip side, adapting your products and services to the special needs of an overseas market is also a proven route to international success.

- **Delivery innovation.** Finding an innovative way to distribute your product or service can be game-changing for your company's performance in international markets. Digital technologies have made it easier than ever before to reach out to overseas customers directly, creating many new opportunities, particularly in the services sector.
- **Business model innovation.** New business models have the power to overturn established players and reshape entire industries. Businesses like Amazon, AirBnB, Google and Uber have revolutionised entire industries with powerful digital platforms that can be used to deliver a whole range of products while sidestepping traditional distribution channels. Yet some of the most effective business model innovations are refinements of existing strengths, rather than revolutionary new methods of doing business. If you already have a great business model, think about which aspects of it could be tweaked to reach new customers overseas.
- **Marketing innovation.** Making sure that your marketing appeals to customers in new markets is essential to international success. Although this takes some work, innovation in international marketing is easier and less expensive than ever before, thanks to digital technologies and social media.
- **Financing innovation.** Securing finance for international ventures is a key challenge for many small companies. But innovative finance methods are becoming increasingly popular and creating new opportunities for international businesses. For example, a growing number of startups are using crowdfunding: raising capital directly from the public, usually via websites and social media channels.

Increased company value

Lastly, nothing increases the value of your company like an international footprint. When a management team can demonstrate to investors that it is selling internationally, or has a clear strategy to reach into multiple markets, they have already flagged the potential for making a lot more money, for all the reasons that I have mentioned. Simply put, companies with international reach have an unfair advantage over their domestic cousins.

CHAPTER 2

THE BELL CURVE IS REAL

CHAPTER 2

THE BELL CURVE IS REAL

Over the years that I have been working with companies going global, I have discovered that the bell curve is real. Every last one of those companies is in one of four places.

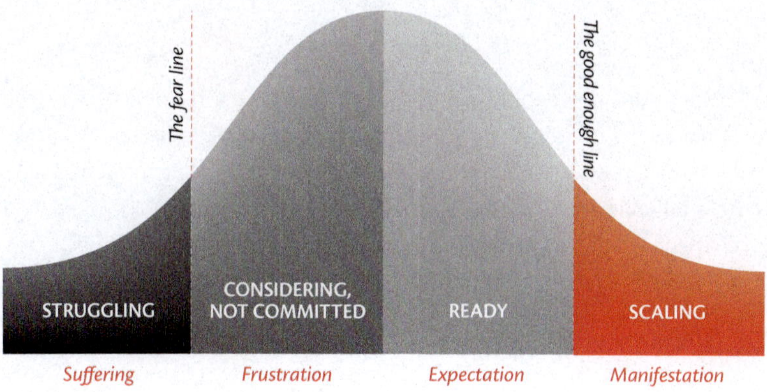

Frustrated and stretched

What I have noticed is that the people who are down the black end of the bell curve are either frustrated or stretched by international expansion.

This is because they have either seen a great opportunity but have not worked out how to grasp it or, because they have jumped into going global without a plan (often to try and shore up flagging revenue at home), and it has not gone well. In both cases, the company leaders do not have a strategy, momentum is low and they often feel like they are going backwards. Revenue is below expectation. Quite frankly, this is a hard place to be.

Between the black and dark grey zones is a hard line that we will call ***the fear line***. A bunch of myths exist at the fear line. People say things to themselves like:

"I don't know where to start, therefore I shouldn't start at all."

This is definitely a myth. If you do not know how to do something, the solution is to figure out how to do it, or to pay someone to do it for you.

"We tried it once before and it didn't work."

It is entirely possible that when you made your initial attempt at *going global* the concept was sound, but your execution was poor. That is not an insurmountable problem.

"This will be easy."

These are the people who fall in love with big numbers. They get carried away by the prospect of huge markets generating massive turnover and receive a nasty surprise when they discover that scaling internationally is more difficult than they expected.

The truth of the matter is that, wherever you find yourself on the bell curve, there are two halves to the equation:

- **The opportunity itself** – which is often where people get the numbers from
- **Your ability to deliver on the opportunity** – which is when you get paid.

International success is not just about what the money could look like. It is about how *well* you can deliver, and how *fast* you can deliver, in order to get paid.

Considering, not committed

When founders and teams jump the fear line and step into a more considered approach, they are usually thinking about going into international markets, or they have started, using a *toe-in-the water* approach. They are doing a little bit here and a little bit there, without committing to the process.

The many companies in the dark grey zone have a strategy which is incoherent or poorly executed, and sometimes both. Because they are starting and stopping – experimenting with international expansion rather than committing to it – it is a struggle to build up any real momentum. Leaders in these companies often feel as though they are spinning their wheels and cannot understand why. Lack of a sound strategy, poor execution and low momentum all drag down performance. Cash flow in dark grey companies is usually stagnant.

Is this as good as it gets?

There is another large group of companies in the light grey zone, which are also average, but on the right side of average. These companies are ready to scale internationally, usually have a plan in place, but may not be executing against it very well.

Sometimes they are already selling into international markets and gaining some momentum, but if they were a Formula 1 car, they would be doing laps of the track at 50 km/h. Revenue at light grey companies is usually positive but uninspiring. Leaders often have a sneaking suspicion that they could be getting better results from their international business.

Some teams in the light grey space find themselves bumping up against the line that separates the light grey and red parts of the bell curve – what I like to call ***the good enough line***. Plenty of people in the light grey part of the curve get there and become complacent because they feel comfortable. They say things to themselves like,:

"Perhaps this is the best we can do."

"Maybe this is as good as it gets."

There are also complacent people who want to jump to the red end of the curve who say:

"If we just keep doing what we've been doing, it'll be fine – more of the same will get us there."

The truth is that while this approach might work in the domestic market, it will not work in global markets. In global markets, the game is so much more complex and the stakes are so much higher. You are dealing with different countries, different banking and legal systems, different cultures, foreign exchange etc. The logistics of transacting business in the international space are far more multifaceted than anything you will deal with at home.

Already expanding

Companies that jump the good enough line and make it to the red part of the bell curve have reached a point where they are already scaling internationally. Teams at these companies have a crystal-clear strategy which they are executing at high speed and revenue is growing. International expansion is an absolute reality for these companies and leaders are asking:

"How do we make the curve turn upwards more sharply – towards 10x?"

These people are often looking for speed and leverage.

Jumping the good enough line is actually about momentum and confidence – knowing that your strategy is sound and that you are good to go. And the red area is largely about ongoing execution at a high standard.

What stops companies going red?

Aside from fear, ignorance, lack of a strategy, lack of funds and sloppy execution, what stops companies from arriving at the red end of the bell curve?

I want to share with you some of the specific mistakes that I see company leaders make around going global. There are many others, but you *must* avoid these three big mistakes to create a great international business:

LACK OF CLARITY

The first mistake that I see people making all the time is that they do not have clarity about what they want to achieve internationally, why they want to go global and how it fits in with their overall strategy.

'THIS WILL BE EASY'

CEOs who have never done it before tend to imagine that going global is easy, because they believe that doing business overseas is just like doing business at home. They underestimate the complexity of selling internationally. They do not realise that their product or service may not suit the international market they plan to target, that their message may not resonate with consumers in other countries – even if well-received at home – and that the way business works in other countries is different. Most importantly, they often fail to understand that you cannot copy and paste a domestic strategy to an international market and expect it to succeed.

LAUNCH TOO SOON

The third mistake that CEOs and founders make, as they go international, is that they launch before they are ready. These people get started without making sure that they have the knowledge, the team and the systems in place to make the international venture a success. As a result, they waste a huge amount of time, energy and money on trying to scale internationally – often with not much to show in the way of results.

So, how do you make sure you get on the path to international success, instead of taking an expensive detour?

CHAPTER 3

THE BLUEPRINT FOR INTERNATIONAL SUCCESS

CHAPTER 3

THE BLUEPRINT FOR INTERNATIONAL SUCCESS

In my experience, the best way to succeed at something you have not tried before is to draw on the experience of those who have. There is no need to reinvent the wheel. After years of working with companies that were going global and conversations with dozens of internationally successful executives, I came up with the ***The Blueprint for International Success*** – my roadmap to take companies international with minimum stress and maximum impact.

The centre of The Blueprint is the goal: to scale internationally and amplify your impact. Playing a bigger game is what it is all about – solving larger problems, helping more people and being paid well to do it along the way.

To scale internationally, you need these three ingredients:

- **10 x Strategy** – a strategy that is likely ten times better than what you currently have, that can take you into international markets and addresses the challenges that you will face along the way
- **10 x Momentum** – you need to be moving ten times faster than you are now
- **10 x Cash flow** – cash in the bank that is increasing at least 10% year on year.

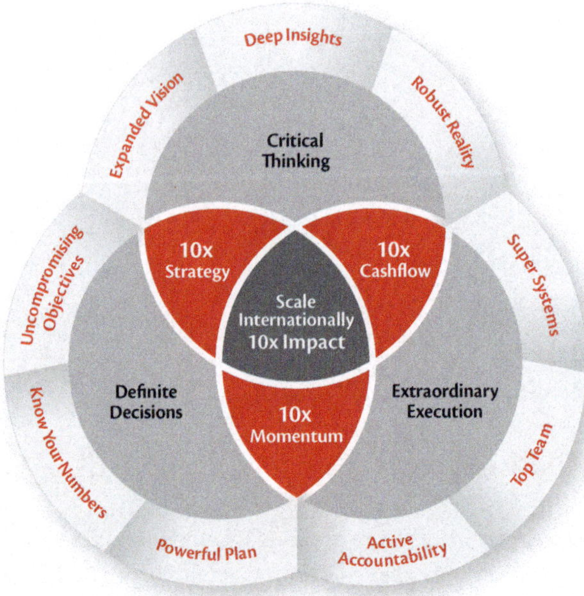

The Blueprint for International Success

With these elements in place, you will find yourself in a much stronger position to scale internationally and to create ten times more impact than you have right now.

To create a 10x strategy, 10x momentum 10x cash flow, you need to pull these three levers:

CRITICAL THINKING

Critical thinking for international markets is different to critical thinking for the domestic market because the stakes are higher and the challenges harder. To think critically for the international space you need to have:

- **Expanded Vision:** A big picture vision rather than a 'nickel and dime' concept of what you want to achieve. This is not the place for 'thinking small'.

- **Deep Insights:** Having deep insights about the markets you are heading to – the people, the culture, the dynamics, the demand – is key to successful critical thinking. The starting point is asking the right questions and getting the right answers to them. Without deep insights, you are almost guaranteed to end up way off track when it comes to developing a strategy.
- **Robust Reality:** As I mentioned earlier, a key piece of creating a successful international strategy is proving feasibility. You need to know if you can actually deliver the promise that you have sold to people and that the company is set up to do it.

DEFINITE DECISIONS

As well as the ability to think critically about your international expansion, your success will be determined by your ability to make definite decisions – high quality decisions that you stick to. Three things that accelerate your ability to make these sorts of decisions are:

- **Knowing Your Numbers:** Knowing your numbers means having hard data and numbers about the performance of your own organisation – especially financial and marketing data – and the country you are planning to sell to, so that you can make decisions based on evidence, not guesswork. It also includes a detailed understanding of what kind of financial resources will be required to make your vision a reality, and how to acquire them.
- **Uncompromising Objectives:** These are goals which are achievable but take you beyond your comfort zone. Uncompromising objectives are vitally important for any business leader planning an international scale-up, because if you remain in your comfort zone with easy goals, you will not grow large enough or fast enough for international success to become a reality.
- **Powerful Plan:** This is a step-by-step plan which sets out what you need to do to make your vision a reality.

EXTRAORDINARY EXECUTION

There are three things that accelerate your ability to execute your vision to a high standard. These are:

- **Super Systems:** When you are scaling internationally and running a business at home, time is one of your most valuable assets. You need high quality systems in place to reduce the time you and your team spend on day-to-day operations and increase the amount of time you can spend on high-value activities like strategic thinking.
- **Top Team:** You also need a team of people (at home and overseas) who buy into your vision, understand their role in making it a reality and are empowered and equipped to make it happen.
- **Cultural Competence:** You and your team need to understand the culture of the new countries you are targeting – how people think, what matters to them, and what they expect from you. Without this, there is huge potential for miscommunication and relationship breakdown.

In the following chapters we will explore each of these elements in more detail. Before we get there, let's talk about time.

Time always wins

On the ***Four Futures Model***, on the next page, you will see that today you are at the location marked 'today'.

Like it or not, if you are reading this book and seriously considering going global (or wanting to do it better), you are on one of the four lines: you are either frustrated or stretched, still considering it, ready to go or already expanding.

In 12 to 24 months, unless you do something different, you will be on the same line. Or worse, you will have dropped down a line and find yourself going backwards.

Getting onto the dark grey and black zones is a function of drift – just drifting along and not taking the action you need to take. And getting onto

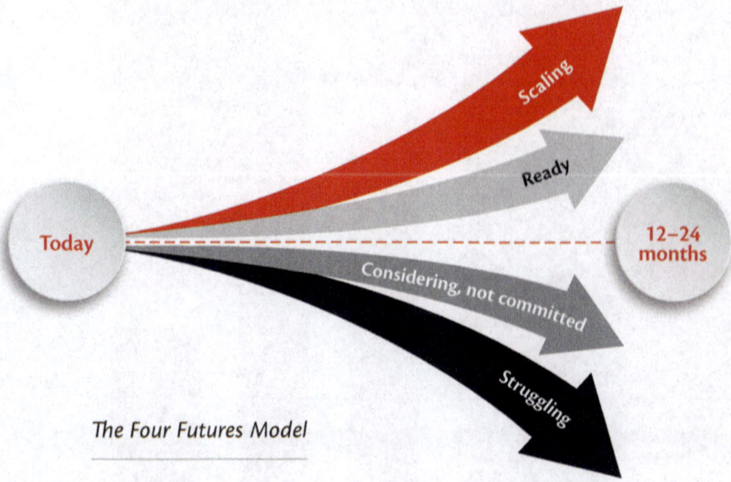

The Four Futures Model

the light grey and red zones are the result of making decisions about what you want to do, taking the right steps and being consistent.

But, if you do it the right way, it's not that hard to end up on one of the upper zones. International expansion is a big project. You need to commit to it for at least a year or two, but I have seen companies jump the line and start gaining momentum even within 90 days.

As a business owner going global, a key question is,

"How long do we want to leave it before we get onto the red line?"

CHAPTER 4

‘SPOILED FOR CHOICE’ – HOW DO WE CHOOSE THE RIGHT MARKET?

CHAPTER 4

'SPOILED FOR CHOICE' – HOW DO WE CHOOSE THE RIGHT MARKET?

You have decided to do it. You are 'going global'. You feel ready, your company seems ready, and your team backs you. So... what next?

Early on in the process you will need to decide where you will sell to. Choosing a market is a key decision, because it shapes so much of what you do subsequently, to prepare to launch internationally.

There is a lot of choice out there when it comes to potential markets, and before you can do much in the way of developing a strategy, you need to decide *where* you are expanding to and *why*.

This is one of the most important decisions you will make on your international journey and getting it wrong can have dramatic consequences, so it is worth putting in some effort.

Alan Oppenheim, CEO of Australian skincare company, Ego Pharmaceuticals, which generates more than 50% of its sales from international markets says:

> *"We know launching into a new country is a really big effort for a whole suite of people, so we look at a whole host of things. We look at what's the population size, what's the GDP, is the GDP growing,*

what's the size of the middle class? Is the middle class growing? Because if people are improving their lives through the economy, then we can help them improve their lives as well, through the science of healthy skin.... So we look at all of that – what's the market for our products? What's the competition like in that country?

"Are there some strange things in the market, where we think the science is wrong, but to enter the market you have to comply with that strange cultural law? What is the culture like? We look at regulations because we're a pharmaceutical company, so we usually have to register the company with the health department first, then every product individually. And that can be a smallish job, or an enormous job. For example, in Saudi Arabia, that took ten years, from my first visit to when we launched – ten years of regulatory work.

"So, there's a whole suite of stuff we look at and one of the things we look at is synergy. If we launch in a particular country, is that going to strengthen the countries around it in synergy? For example, Singapore and Malaysia are different, but they are physically connected, so there is some synergy between the two. And we are re finding the more countries we are in, the more synergies there are across the world."

In case you are wondering what *getting it wrong* looks like, let me share a few of the big mistakes that I see people make all the time as they launch into international markets.

How businesses get it wrong

AD HOC DECISIONS

You would be blown away by the number of people who make ad hoc decisions about which country to expand to – either because they went on holiday somewhere and fell in love with it, they received a random order from a new market or they have heard that there are 'big opportunities' there.

Let me illustrate. If you have been in business a while, the chances are that you have been randomly contacted by potential customers from overseas who wanted to work with you or place an order with your firm. It is very easy to get excited and carried away at this point, especially if the order is from a country where you believe there is a massive potential market for your product.

Before you rush to fill it and before you start dreaming about becoming a market leader in that country, take the time to work out whether your offering really belongs in that market and whether going there really fits with your company's broader strategic priorities. If not, do not waste your time, especially if there is no indication that the initial, random order is going to turn into anything more permanent.

NO REAL RESEARCH

Research is not loads of fun, and it takes a real investment of time and energy. That is one reason that so many people do not do real research before they choose an international market to target.

I worked with a company a couple of years ago that was planning its internationalisation and export play primarily around selling into China. The product was hydroponic fruit and vegetables and the rationale for going into China went something like this:

> *"We know China is a huge market and we know that its middle class is growing rapidly. We know that the middle class wants premium products and does not trust domestically produced food. We will sell our premium fresh food into China and exploit that market."*

Superficially, this seemed like a pretty sound argument and on the strength of it the company had decided that it would target China to the exclusion of other overseas markets. What its leadership team did not know was that there was no market access to China, because China only allows a handful of fruit and vegetable products to be imported from abroad. Legally, the company had no ability to sell its products in the Chinese market ... and that was the end of that expansion strategy.

I have met plenty of people who snatched at the first proposition that came along, rather than choosing a market rationally, on the basis of research. It often ends badly, because what appears to be a great opportunity at first glance just does not stack up on closer examination. Maybe the size of the market is not what you imagined, or the competition in your sector is fierce. Perhaps the customers cannot pay what you need to charge to make a profit or the banking system is not sophisticated enough to support your business model. Or maybe you have discovered that the culture of your target market does not gel with you – you do not like the food, the people seem rude, and you hate having to travel 12 hours to do business there every six weeks.

UNDERESTIMATING THE COMPLEXITY OF ENTERING A NEW MARKET

When you have not taken the time to do your research thoroughly, many countries seem similar at first glance. They have similar languages, currencies, transport systems and hotel lobbies. However, every market has its own practices; some of them are cultural, others are mandated by law.

It is not always easy to discern these differences from the outside. Business people often make the mistake of assuming that selling in a particular market will be straightforward, because it appears to be similar to their home market, or to another country that they are already selling to. As you scratch the surface, you may discover that your target market is far less simple to work in than you would have imagined.

Making assumptions about the ease or difficulty of working in or selling to a particular place is, a recipe for running into all kinds of obstacles that you had not even imagined, from unexpected customer preferences, to snags with packaging and labelling requirements; from problems with getting your product onto the shelves of a local supermarket, to difficulties in firing an underperforming distributor; from hassles with setting up bank accounts to challenges with getting paid on time – or at all – by your clients.

TRYING TO ENTER MORE THAN ONE MARKET AT ONE TIME

I liken this mistake to trying to light multiple fires with one magnifying glass.

Depending on what type of business you run and how you decide to enter the market, trying to go into more than one market at a time is distracting at best and suicidal at worst.

If you are new to international business, selling to, or setting up, in multiple countries when you first expand overseas is more or less guaranteed to break your company unless it is already reasonably large and/or highly successful at home. The exception to this rule might be Saas (software as a service) products or small items that can be sent directly to several markets by a platform like Amazon or by courier.

It is not worth getting it wrong!

No matter how amazing the rush of making a quick, 'gut feel' decision to sell to a particular place feels, it is not worth getting it wrong, because the consequences of making a poor choice of market are serious.

In the short-term you will waste resources, time and energy that you could have invested in a venture that would create better outcomes for you and your company. If things do not go to plan and the venture performs worse than expected, you might experience cash flow problems and there will certainly be an opportunity cost, which could sour the prospect of expanding internationally in the future.

The longer-term consequences of a poor choice of market can be much grimmer (particularly if you make your mistake on a large scale) and can include damage to your brand and a downgrade and a depreciation in the value of your company. This really matters if you are planning a future exit via a trade sale.

How do we get it right?

In a word, the answer is 'research'. Choosing the right market is not rocket science. It takes some work, but if you do your homework before you reach any conclusions about which market is right for your company to expand to, you will be in a much better position to know which decision is the right one. Here is why.

REAL DATA AND EVIDENCE-BASED DECISIONS

When you carry out real research on international markets, you have real data to back you up. That means that rather than going purely on 'gut feel' (which I do not recommend), you are empowered with the information to make evidence-based decisions that make commercial sense. Both the data and the confidence it gives will help you to get clarity about which international market is right for your company.

Armed with clarity and confidence, you can start planning your international strategy quickly and from a solid foundation. And that is a much better way to start than jumping in with your eyes closed.

CASE STUDY: Peter Geoghegan, Geotron

Peter Geoghegan came to the International Business Accelerator (which my company runs for small businesses) for help with expanding his young engineering consulting firm, Geotron, overseas. Here is what he says about selecting a market:

"I had lots of drive and inspiration to take the company offshore in Asia, but one of my biggest early challenges was deciding where to go. I was tossing up between half-a-dozen different markets and wondering whether I should tackle several at the same time. It was an overwhelming prospect and I started to wonder whether or not I really could succeed internationally, or whether it was just some kind of a crazy pipe-dream.

"When I had done research on all the places I was thinking of going to and crunched the numbers, things started to fall into

place. I could see that some markets, like Indonesia and China had huge potential, but were also going to be challenging to work in, whereas others, like Singapore and Malaysia, were smaller, but more manageable for a boutique firm like ours. I also realised that it was okay to take things slowly and tackle one country at a time, rather than stressing myself out by trying to enter multiple markets simultaneously and spreading our small team too thin.

"A year on, we're setting up the firm in Singapore, we've acquired two major multinationals as clients, and we've concluded a strategic alliance with a third. I think focusing on just one country has helped us consolidate our efforts quickly and I'm surprised by how far we've come in a short time, especially when you consider that twelve months ago, I wasn't even sure which country we should start with or whether an international expansion was something we could achieve".

Choosing a market

DECIDE HOW TO CHOOSE

There are a variety of different ways that you can go about choosing an international market to sell to or expand to.

- As I mentioned earlier, many people consider exporting or expanding in response to enquiries from potential customers overseas.
- Alternatively, you might decide to focus on markets that are close to your home market and culturally and economically quite similar. This reduces the likelihood that you will have to deal with huge differences in culture, regulations, customer expectations or economic structures.
- You could also target countries which have sizeable populations and national wealth, where consumers are already familiar with and using products like yours.

- Perhaps you choose a country where you already have strong relationships, built through study, work or family ties. You believe you can build on those and that foundation of familiarity and trust becomes a key driver for your choice of destination.
- Or you might decide to look for opportunities in completely new markets where you believe that you have a strong competitive advantage because, for example, no-one else sells a product or service like yours.

Each of these methods has its pros and cons: none of them are necessarily better than others, provided that you can justify your decision. In the end, how you decide to choose a country to sell to will depend on what you want to achieve. Even so, it is a good idea to be clear on how you are going to choose a market, as doing so will help you to develop criteria for evaluating markets – you won't be just jumping in blind.

DO YOUR RESEARCH

No matter how you decide to choose, thorough market research is essential. The challenge here is knowing how much and what kind of research to do. The two common extremes are:

- Doing virtually no research at all and making a poor choice of market
- Getting stuck in research mode and using it to delay taking action.

You might be wondering, "*What is the minimum amount of research that I need to do?*" but a better question is, "*What is the minimum I need to know?*"

The most important question that you need to be able to answer is, "*Will people in this country buy what I am selling?*" but there are some other key considerations that you should take into account as you go about selecting a market to sell to. The rest of this chapter addresses those questions.

GET A 30,000 FOOT VIEW

To get an initial idea of which countries are the best candidates for you to consider as destinations for your international expansion, you should consider:

- Which countries have the largest and fastest growing markets for my product?
- Which countries might be profitable markets for my product/service?
- Which foreign markets will be the easiest to enter?

Once you have answered these questions, you should have a group of markets that you can choose from.

For each of the markets that you think you want to go to, you need to answer the following questions:

WHAT IS THE SIZE OF THE OPPORTUNITY?

To discover the size of the opportunity for your company in a market, you will need to know how many people in that country would want to buy your product or, alternatively, what percentage of market share you think you could capture if there were no competitors. This is called calculating your 'total addressable market' (TAM). It is important to get a handle on the size of the market you are planning to target. Knowing the size of the TAM will give you an objective point of comparison with other markets. It will also help you as you go about estimating how many extra units of your product or service you will need to create in that market over time, and what resources you will require to do so.

You also need to know whether people in your target country can afford your products and whether they are likely to pay a premium for them. The answers to these questions are linked to the levels of income in your chosen country, region or area, so it is helpful to gather information on how much the average person in that country earns, how much the customers you are targeting earn and what people in that country typically spend their money on.

You should also research your industry sector. Is it booming in the country you are considering or is it one that is still developing? Could you gain a first mover advantage? How does the size of your target market compare to that of another country? Where is the greatest commercial opportunity?

WHAT ABOUT THE DEMOGRAPHICS?

It is worth checking out the demographics of markets you are considering, to get an idea of the age, gender and spread of the population. This can provide clues about the state of the economy. For instance, with some exceptions, countries with young populations are more likely to have economies that are growing than countries that have ageing populations.

Demographics can also indicate whether there is likely to be demand for your offering in a particular country. For example, products and services aimed at babies and toddlers (daycare centres, baby formula, toys) are likely to be in greater demand in a country with a young, growing population than in a country with an ageing, declining population. Conversely, if you are selling aged care services, you probably want to target a country where the average age is over 37 and birth rates are falling, rather than a country where more than 50% of the population is under 25 years of age and birth rates are steady or rising. Why? Because the first country is likely to have many elderly people and fewer young people to take care of them, which means that the elderly are more likely to need aged care services. The second country probably has fewer elderly people and a ready supply of young people who can care for them and bear the cost of public-provided aged care services, through the taxes they pay.

Demographics can also help you to decide where, within a particular country, to focus your attention. In many countries, most people tend to live around major cities and capitals, so these can be a good place to start. If your business is more likely to appeal to customers across the whole of a country, or in remote areas where population density (and therefore the volume of potential clients) is lower, you will need to think about how you will reach them and the cost per opportunity.

WHO IS OUR COMPETITION?

Before you draw a conclusion about which country is the right place for you to start your international expansion, you need to get a handle on the competition.

A good place to start is by finding out whether your competitors in your home market are working internationally and where they are selling to. If you can find out how they are performing in that country, even better. Their website, press releases and business news should give you some clues. Then you have to decide whether you want to compete with them, or choose to develop your business in another country where they have not established a base.

It is likely that aside from the competitors you are already aware of, there are many competitors you have not even considered. These companies might be local, or they might be global operations with a foothold in the country you are targeting. You need to understand who these competitors are and assess what kind of threat they pose to you. This is significant because if you are thinking of entering a particular market and it turns out that there are numerous competitors already selling the same thing as your product, you may be in for a tough time. This can be true even if your product has features that you believe differentiate it from competitor products.

If you discover that your preferred country already has several competitors playing in your space, you will need to think long and hard about whether you are offering anything unique or different to the competition. You also need to consider how you will capture market share, as it can be difficult to win customers away from competitors who are already providing a good product or service.

ARE THERE ANY BARRIERS TO TRADING WITH THIS COUNTRY?

One of the key questions you need to answer as you size up a country as an expansion destination is,

"Are there any barriers to trading with this country?"

There may be obvious deal-breakers such as a trade embargo or sanctions, but there are other factors to consider too. I have listed some of the most important ones here.

POLITICAL STABILITY OF THE MARKET AND REGION

Political instability in a country or region (coups, multiple rapid changes of government, popular uprisings, civil war, conflicts with neighbouring countries) can have a dramatic impact on general business confidence, investor sentiment, and your ability to do business there.

The effects of political strife can range from bureaucratic obstacles, such as border taxes and trade embargoes, to disruptions in transport networks that threaten supply chains, or property losses that force a halt in trading or production.

The spat between Qatar and the other Arab Gulf States, which started in 2017 and began to resolve in late 2020, is a case in point. Suspended land, sea and air links with Qatar had an immediate impact on businesses and individuals alike. Shipping costs increased tenfold after the UAE restricted access to its ports for ships transporting goods to Qatar and services professionals from abroad were also badly affected. For William Grieve, a Bahrain-based businessman with consulting work in Manama and Doha, his weekly 40-minute flight to Qatar became a 10-hour journey via Kuwait[6].

Political instability can also reduce customer demand, and make it harder to secure financing, obtain insurance or settle bad debts. It is also likely to affect the host country currency, potentially reducing the value of assets invested in that country, along with future profits generated by them[7].

In the last decade, emerging markets, in particular, have experienced diverse changes in their political stability, with important implications for business environments and economic growth. In countries like Indonesia and Chile, improvements in political stability and the business environment have boosted investor confidence and led to increased foreign direct investment (FDI), while in places like Egypt and Ukraine, persistent political turmoil has shaken investor and consumer confidence.

Political stability is also worth keeping in mind because it tends to be linked to the business environment, particularly in emerging markets. Emerging markets which are politically stable – such as the UAE, Chile, Hungary and Poland – often offer favourable business environments for firms. That is because good governance facilitates reforms and investments.

This does not mean that you should never consider operating in a politically unstable region – companies like Haliburton, Kellogg Brown & Root (KBR) and numerous security firms made fortunes in Iraq and Afghanistan during the early 2000s, specifically because they offered services that were in high demand in politically volatile places. However, if you do want to target a politically unstable market, think carefully about what kind of risks political instability might generate for your business; whether you have the appetite to deal with those risks; and how you will mitigate and manage risk as it arises. Political instability in an area where a firm operates will mean that the company has to be very flexible and adaptable – ready to change its operations at very short notice to reflect changes in the political environment.

ARE THERE POLITICAL RISKS?

Even in countries which seem politically stable, political change can have a significant impact on business. Change can occur when the government changes the legal framework, but it could also be that a change of government changes political attitudes towards business, with flow-on consequences.

For example, trade tensions between the US and China escalated dramatically after maverick Republican Party nominee Donald Trump became President of the United States. Trump's pivot on trade policy aggravated China's ruling party. As the conflict deepened, both countries imposed tariffs on a wide range of goods including steel and aluminium, pork, fruit and nuts, steel pipe for the oil industry, and ethanol, to name just a handful of items[8].

The US government also banned US companies in some sectors, including ICT, from working with Chinese companies, putting partnerships at risk. The most high-profile of these was the partnership between

Google and Chinese company ZTE Corp. ZTE was working with Google to manufacture a low-cost Android phone, which would have put Google's Android technology into the hands of millions of less-affluent smartphone users around the world[9].

Trade conflicts can also have less obvious consequences for companies doing international business. A colleague of mine ran a craft beer business in California. He was negotiating with investors to expand the brand into China by establishing a number of breweries across the country, when the US-China trade tensions blew up early in 2018. Investing into foreign joint ventures became a 'sensitive' topic in some Chinese provinces and investors became concerned that they might be sanctioned for dealing with American firms while the disputes were ongoing. They were also concerned about the impact of the tariffs on the cost of producing the beer. Both of the groups which had planned to fund breweries in China decided to pause progress for at least six months, as a result of which the client's crowdfunding round collapsed. His company ended up filing for bankruptcy.

Governments can also change the social agenda and this may impact foreign firms. For example, a government may introduce, or modify, a minimum wage. Or it may sign on to international agreements that affect employee terms and conditions and significantly increase the costs of doing business in that country. As you choose a market, inform yourself about what is happening there politically and how political changes could affect your company if you choose to go there.

REGULATORY FRAMEWORKS

Take a look at the regulatory frameworks of the markets you think you want to go to. Companies in any country operate within a governance framework which is set by national laws, regulations and codes of best practice.

The structure and operation of a country's regulatory environment can have a big impact on how easy it is for your company to do business there. A weak or badly-managed regulatory framework can increase the costs and risks of doing business, create difficulties in hiring foreign workers and make it hard to get trade finance, to give just a few examples.

Specific topics that you can research to understand a market's regulatory framework include finding out how easy it is to:

- Start a business in your target market
- Register property
- Get electricity
- Obtain credit
- Protect investors
- Pay taxes
- Trade across borders
- Enforce contracts
- Manage insolvency.

The World Bank's annual *Doing Business* report is a great place to start.

NON-TARIFF BARRIERS

A non-tariff barrier (NTB) is any measure, other than a customs tariff, that acts as a barrier to international trade. Unlike tariffs, NTBs are not necessarily quantifiable or measurable and are often hidden.

Sometimes referred to as 'red tape', NTBs are often part of a country's regulatory framework and typically include quotas, boycotts, licences, standards and regulations, local content requirements, restrictions on foreign investment, domestic government purchasing policies, exchange controls, and subsidies.

NTBs can be more restrictive for trade than actual tariffs. With the exception of a few sensitive products where tariffs remain high, it is NTBs that are the real impediment to international trade today. That is a great reason to research potential NTBs when you are choosing an export market – you do not want to be caught out. Non-tariff barriers to trade include:

- **Licences:** A licence is granted to a business by the government and allows the business to operate or import goods into the country. For example, in most countries, professionals including engineers, lawyers and doctors require licences to practice, and professional firms including engineering consultancies, law firms and medical practices require licences to operate. These licences are usually more difficult to acquire if the professional obtained their qualifications in another country or the principals of the firm are not resident or qualified in that country. This creates a restriction on competition from overseas firms.

- **Import Quotas:** An import quota is a restriction placed on the amount of a particular good that can be imported. For example, a country may place a quota on the volume of imported citrus fruit that is allowed.
- **Voluntary Export Restraints (VER):** This type of trade barrier is 'voluntary' in that it is created by the exporting country rather than the importing one. A voluntary export restraint is usually levied at the behest of the importing country and could be accompanied by a reciprocal VER. For example, Brazil could place a VER on the exportation of sugar to Canada, based on a request by Canada. Canada could then place a VER on the exportation of coal to Brazil. This increases the price of both coal and sugar but protects the domestic industries.
- **Local Content Requirements:** Instead of placing a quota on the number of goods that can be imported, the government can require that a certain percentage of a good be made domestically. The restriction can be a percentage of the good itself or a percentage of the value of the good. For example, a restriction on the import of computers might say that 25% of the pieces used to make the computer are made domestically, or that 15% of the value of the good must come from domestically produced components.

TARIFFS

In basic terms, a tariff is a tax that adds to the cost of imported goods. Governments levy tariffs to provide revenue for the government. Tariffs also protect domestic firms from foreign competition, by making it more expensive for foreign companies to sell their goods in the domestic market.

There are several types of tariffs and barriers that a government can employ.

- **Specific Tariffs:** A specific tariff is a fixed fee levied on one unit of an imported good. This tariff can vary according to the type of good imported. For example, a country could levy a $15 tariff on each pair of shoes imported, but levy a $300 tariff on each computer imported.
- **Ad Valorem Tariffs:** The phrase ad valorem is Latin for 'according to value,' and this type of tariff is levied on a good based on a percentage of that good's value. An example of an ad valorem tariff would be a 15% tariff levied by Japan on US automobiles. The 15% is a price increase on the value of the automobile, so a $10,000 vehicle now costs $11,500 to Japanese consumers. This price increase protects domestic producers from being undercut but also keeps prices artificially high for Japanese car shoppers.

Before you go ahead and choose a market, find out whether there are any tariffs that apply to the products that you sell. If there are, you will need to factor that into the end price that your international customers will pay and work out whether you can still sell your product at a price point that makes sense.

FREE TRADE AGREEMENTS

As you consider which country might be right for your company to expand to, it is worth checking whether there is a free trade agreement (FTA) between your home market and the market you are targeting. FTAs can provide you with a competitive edge over companies from other countries which are also targeting the market.

FTAs are designed to reduce the barriers to trade (typically tariffs and trade quotas) between two or more countries. When countries sign an FTA, they agree to give preferential access to each other's markets by exempting each other from the tariffs and quotas that apply to countries that are not party to the agreement. This could mean that tariffs and quotas are reduced or removed entirely. For example, the Australia-Japan FTA will cut Japan's tariff on Australian beef from 38.5% to 19.5% over 18 years. The agreement allows Australian beef producers to sell their product in Japan with 50% less tariff cost than producers from countries that have not negotiated a preferential rate with Japan.

FTAs also try to reduce non-tariff barriers by:

- Seeking to reduce the cost to business of complying with multiple regulations
- Banning discrimination against foreign firms or limits on how much business they can do
- At least partly opening up government purchasing to bids by foreign business
- By requiring countries to have at least a specified level of protection for intellectual property (patents and copyright).

If there is an FTA between your home market and the market you are trying to enter, it is worth finding out how the agreement applies to your industry and how you can use it to your advantage.

CASE STUDY: Della Rosa Pizza

Emilio de Lorso started his first business in 1990, making pizza bases with his mum in their garage. His company, Della Rosa, has since become a leading Australian production facility, which employs more than 230 people and sells nationally and internationally.

As Emilio started to export his ready-made pizzas to the world, the price of pizza was initially a big problem. When he visited China, Emilio found pizzas to be amongst the most expensive products in the supermarket. However, when the China-Australia Free Trade Agreement came into force, the situation improved significantly. Tariffs on pizza toppings fell from 10% to 4%, reducing the cost of Della Rosa pizzas by 60% in the Chinese market and making the company far more competitive[10]*. These days Della Rosa is a leading player in its segment in China.*

INTELLECTUAL PROPERTY PROTECTION

Knowing whether you will be able to protect your intellectual property (IP) in any country you do business in is a crucial consideration. For example, there is not much point selling your state-of-the-art medical device into China (which is notorious for high rates of IP theft and copy-catting) if you know that the device will be copied, manufactured and sold to your potential client for a fraction of its real value by a Chinese competitor. It is even worse if there is nothing you can do to address and redress the theft of your IP.

IP frameworks vary wildly from place to place. As a starting point, check whether your target market is covered by international IP conventions, such as the Madrid International Trademark System. That way, you will be aware of what protections are available if your IP is infringed in a foreign market.

If the market you are targeting has an FTA in place with your home country, this agreement may also provide additional protection for your IP.

I will cover intellectual property in more detail in Chapter 14.

INFRASTRUCTURE

Depending on the business you are in, the quality of a country's infrastructure could be a defining factor in how easy it is for you to do business there and how likely you are to succeed in that market.

'Infrastructure' is an umbrella term for a nation's basic physical systems – for example transportation, communication, sewage, water and electricity – which can have a positive or negative impact on your ability to do business there.

Poor countries often suffer from a low level of trade-related infrastructure, such as telecommunications and transportation, which can make doing business in those places hard.

Inadequate road, rail, sea or air transportation networks can be a brake on trade, especially when moving goods across a large territory from inland facilities to coastal ports. For example, significant opportunities exist to export halal beef and lamb products into markets in the Middle East, but not all countries in the region have the infrastructure to readily store and transport chilled or frozen meat products once they arrive at a seaport or airport. While the United Arab Emirates is well-equipped with good roads and sophisticated cold supply-chain facilities, countries like Egypt, or even the UAE's near neighbour Kuwait, have limited cold storage facilities and underdeveloped transport infrastructure, which makes supplying large volumes of meat to those countries a challenge.

Unreliable communications and technology infrastructure can also add uncertainty to a company's supply chain by, for example, making it difficult to track containers at ports or forcing shippers to rely on paper documentation instead of electronic customs processing.

Infrastructure also includes so-called 'soft' infrastructure – institutions such as the healthcare system, financial institutions, governmental systems, law enforcement and education systems that help maintain the economy. These usually require human capital and help deliver certain services to the population.

If you are planning to work in a country with weak 'soft infrastructure', think about how this might affect your business. You may find it challenging to repatriate capital if financial institutions are not robust. If you run into a legal dispute, obtaining and enforcing judgements in your favour could be a lot more difficult if the country's legal frameworks and processes are not transparent. If you are thinking about going somewhere with a patchy education system and low levels of general education, consider whether you will be able to find qualified staff to work for you in-country, or whether you may need to bring in staff with specialist skills from abroad.

DISTRIBUTION CHANNELS

You will also need to think about whether the markets you are considering have the appropriate distribution channels in place to let you get your products and services to the market. This might seem straightforward in a developed economy, but it is not always the case.

Let us suppose you sell software, online games or other virtual products that require lots of bandwidth and high download speeds to get them into the end user's hands. Do not hold your breath for stellar adoption rates in Australia, where internet speeds ranked 51st in the world in 2017 and 55th in the world in 2021, despite the fact that the country is a G20 nation.

If you are selling physical goods, how will you get them into the customer's hands? Suppose you want to keep costs low by avoiding distributors and selling directly to customers. If you are targeting the enormous Chinese middle-class market, you could investigate using the Chinese *daigou*[11] network and WeChat to reach them. But what if you are selling to Indonesia, which has millions of consumers, fragmented distribution channels and no *daigou* network?

How you choose to distribute your products and services can have a big impact on the speed of delivery, end price and general customer experience, so make sure that wherever you are going, you will be able to access distribution channels that make sense for your company.

TIME DIFFERENCE

This one might seem bizarre, but it does matter. As you choose a market to expand to, keep time zones in mind. A big time difference between your hometown and your target market or the location of your team members can make life difficult.

Time differences become challenging wherever human interaction is involved, and the bigger the time difference, the more people will be inconvenienced. As the number of time zones your operation crosses approaches the double digits, cultural norms and biological imperatives mean somebody – often the business owner – is working all day, every day. Breakfast in Silicon Valley is dinnertime in London, and Sunday is a working day in Saudi Arabia.

If you are a New Zealand company shipping dairy products to Ethiopia, with no interaction with your Ethiopian customers and only occasional communication with your distributor in-country, a nine-hour time difference may not make much difference. But if you are an Indian company in the call-centre business with customers on the West Coast of the USA, the 12.5-hour time difference between Chennai and San Francisco will be problematic the moment your home team and your US team have to start working together in real-time.

When I worked as a management consultant, I led a team that was split between Washington DC, United States and Baghdad, Iraq. For part of the time that I was leading the team, I was based in Sydney and we were holding team conference calls every second day as an important deadline loomed. For the team members in Washington DC the calls started at 8:00am – not great, but definitely manageable. For the team members in Baghdad, the calls started at 4:00pm – no problem. For me, in Sydney, the calls started at midnight and went through until 2:00am, every second night. The novelty wore off quickly – I was crashing out exhausted and wired at 3:00am every second morning, and arriving back at my desk by 8:00am, just five hours later. After a week, I was feeling a little burnt out. The time difference never became a big problem because the project lasted a relatively short time, but it would have been a different story if I had been a business owner who had to work with that kind of time difference over a long period of time.

A while ago, our US office terminated a contract with a service provider in Pakistan, because the 10-hour time difference was having a negative impact on the turn-around of projects and slowing them down by days. The US team found a new service provider in Jamaica, which has only a two-hour time difference with San Francisco, and the speed and quality of the work product (and the relationship with the provider) improved overnight.

LANGUAGE AND CULTURE

Language and culture may not be 'barriers' to doing business in a particular country, but they can have a significant impact. If you are planning to work and sell in a market where the language and culture are very different to your own, ask yourself whether you are equipped to deal with those differences ... and whether you want to deal with them.

If you are British, have no aptitude for languages, and hate pickled cabbage, entering the South Korean market may not be an experience you enjoy, especially if you must spend a lot of time in Seoul, eating kimchi.

If you are going to build a business in a country which has a different language, consider how you will manage this, as communication across languages and cultures can be fraught with misunderstandings, and there is plenty of potential for conflict in cross-cultural business relationships.

Also think carefully about how prepared you are to invest time and energy into learning about and understanding the customs, beliefs, communication styles and etiquette of the country you are going to. A successful international expansion is going to require you to immerse yourself in your target market, to get to know people, to make friendships, to build alliances and to spend time there. If the culture of a particular place does not gel with you, or you have strong objections about aspects of the culture and government policy, think twice before committing to building a business there.

Can we make a profit?

Once you have come up with a list of countries which seem to make good sense as potential destinations for an international expansion, it is time to get down to the nitty gritty: of the markets you are considering, which one can you make a profit in? This is one of the most important questions you will answer. If you cannot make a profit, there is little point in considering selling to, or setting up in, that country.

To work out whether you can make a profit, you will need to know how much your competitors charge, how much it will cost to distribute your product or service and whether there are any trade barriers that will add to your cost of doing business in that market.

Once you have gathered enough information to build a picture of your target market, established that potential customers in that country want and are likely to pay for what you are selling, and that you can make a profit selling in that country, you are ready to make a decision about whether you want to do business there.

TIPS ON DOING RESEARCH

As I have mentioned numerous times in this chapter, making a good choice about which international market to sell to inevitably involves research.

If you hate research, do not know where to start, or do not have much time, here are some tips to get you going.

- Download free resources from government trade agencies in your home country and the country you are thinking of going to. These can be a great starting point.
- Speak to people who have already tried operating in the market you're planning to enter and find out, first-hand, what has worked and what has not. You can get some incredibly valuable insights from a conversation over a meal.
- Block out specific chunks of time (preferably four hours in a block) to work on your research project. Put it in your diary as an appointment and make sure you keep it.
- Get help. Hire an intern or junior researcher to assist you with finding and compiling data. If you can make the investment, get an expert to create a market report for you – it will cost you, but less than running the same calibre of research yourself.
- If you can, visit. Once you have done enough research to verify that the market you want to enter seems to be the right one, go there. Do not try to do much business on the first visit, just go and make sure that it is somewhere you will enjoy working and that you like interacting with the people. Use the time to set up more meetings and conversations, to confirm and enrich the information that you have unearthed through desk research. Get comfortable and connected with the locals. Then start.

CHAPTER 5 YOUR IDEAL INTERNATIONAL CLIENT

CHAPTER 5

YOUR IDEAL INTERNATIONAL CLIENT

As your business expands overseas, you will want to build relationships with your Ideal International Clients (IIC). These are the prospects most in need of your services, who will get the most value from your offering. They are the customers most likely to buy from you, and most likely to generate maximum revenue for your company over the long term. Being able to locate and speak to these prospects depends on knowing who your Ideal International Client is, what problems they have that you can solve, and where to find them.

Too many companies – including firms that have been selling internationally for some time – have no clear idea about who their IIC is, or what that client wants. They either take a 'one size fits all' approach and hope for the best, assume that international clients will want the same thing as clients at home, or both.

These are problems that no amount of marketing can fix. If you take a general approach and base your strategy for targeting international clients on assumptions, it's likely that neither your offering nor your marketing are going to connect with your ideal client, because you are operating on guesswork. This phenomenon is true in the domestic market and it becomes even more pronounced when you go offshore.

The global marketplace is competitive. Knowing who your IIC is and what they value should drive every facet of your international business.

From the product you offer and how you work with your clients, to the text and images you use on your website and what you post on social media, it all needs to be directly targeted to a specific set of values and desires.

Defining the Ideal International Client

To reach your IICs and solve their problems, you must find out what their problems really are, not just what you *think* they are.

It is not rocket science, but it does take work. The first step is segmentation.

SEGMENTATION

As you expand your business internationally, the number of people you can sell to goes through the roof, and it's likely that you will have more than one ideal client. Segmenting the market allows you to narrow down the ocean of people you could be speaking to and maximise the likelihood that your message will reach people who want to hear from you.

Segmentation is dividing clients into sub-groups based on shared characteristics. When you segment, you recognise differences between groups of customers and identify their needs, enabling you to offer a more personalised and targeted experience. Segmentation also allows you to:

- **Create stronger marketing messages.** By avoiding generic, vague language for a broad audience, you can focus directly on the needs, wants, and unique characteristics of your target audience.
- **Identify the most effective marketing tactics.** When you know the audience you are targeting, you can determine the best solutions and methods for reaching them.
- **Design hyper-targeted ads.** On digital ad services, you can target audiences by their age, location, purchasing habits, interests, and more. When you use market segmentation to define your audience, you know these detailed characteristics and can use them to create more effective, targeted digital ad campaigns.

- **Differentiate your brand from competitors.** Instead of blending in with other brands, you can differentiate your brand by focusing on specific customer needs and characteristics.
- **Build deeper customer affinity.** When you know what your customers want and need, you can deliver and communicate offerings that uniquely serve and resonate with them.
- **Identify niche market opportunities.** Niche marketing is the process of identifying segments of industries and verticals that have a large audience that can be served in new ways. When you segment your target market, you can find underserved niche markets to target with new products and services.
- **Stay focused.** Targeting in marketing keeps your messaging and marketing objectives on track. It helps you identify new marketing opportunities and avoid distractions that will lead you away from your target market.

HOW SHOULD I SEGMENT MY INTERNATIONAL MARKET?

The answer depends on your objectives.

There are as many different types of segmentation as there are goals to be pursued. The first step is to define what you want to achieve. You might be thinking,

"Isn't the real goal always to maximise revenue?"

Of course that is true. In an ideal world, you would segment the market by predicting how much revenue you could expect to earn by converting a prospect into a client and using that prediction to decide which prospects you would pay the most attention to. This is 'tiered segmentation'.

Unfortunately, tiered segmentation is extremely difficult to do well because it's hard to tell exactly how much revenue your company can earn from a given customer. For instance, if you were selling B2B, you would need to know the details of your prospect's future needs, their company's future plans and the dynamics of their industry, and lots of other small details about how they operate.

To do tiered segmentation well, you need to know your prospect's company better than they know it themselves.

Even though you cannot predict exactly how much revenue you will earn from a given customer, you can come up with a few criteria for segmenting the market. This will give you a set of prospects who are more likely to need what you offer and more likely to spend money on what you can do for them.

The four basic segmentation approaches are:

- **Geographic segmentation**
- **Demographic segmentation**
- **Psychographic segmentation**
- **Behavioural segmentation**

Within each of these types of market segmentation, multiple sub-categories further classify audiences and customers. So how do we apply them in different contexts? In this chapter, we will use two Australian examples of companies that are targeting overseas markets: Minnow Designs and Crawford Boots.

Minnow Designs is run by co-founders Lorraine Cherry-Nguyen and Stacey Ellis Fisher. The company makes specialty footwear – swimmable shoes for babies and children – sells B2C and is targeting markets across Asia and the United States.

Crawford Boots is run by Penny Crawford, a podiatrist turned entrepreneur. It sells specialised, waterproof, injury-reducing footwear for people working on wet, unstable surfaces. Its customers are companies that have employees working in those conditions. Crawford Boots is pursuing opportunities in the United States and Canada.

Geographic Segmentation

Geographic segmentation is the simplest type of market segmentation and is an obvious starting point when we are segmenting for international markets, as most businesses will want to begin by targeting one or two specific countries.

Geographic segmentation groups customers based on geographic parameters like:

- Country
- State
- Postcode
- City
- Climate
- Urban or rural
- Radius around a certain location

It can refer to a defined geographic boundary (such as a city or postcode) or type of area (such as the size of city or type of climate).

Minnow Designs will almost certainly segment its markets geographically by targeting customers who spend a lot of time at the beach. This means people who live in warm climates, by the coast.

Crawford Boots will use geographic segmentation to focus their efforts on states in North America where there is a lot of mining activity and where mining companies have chosen to headquarter.

Demographic Segmentation

Demographic segmentation is one of the most popular and commonly used types of market segmentation. In a B2C context, it refers to statistical data about a group of people including:

- Age
- Gender
- Income
- Location
- Family situation
- Education
- Ethnicity

Minnow Designs uses demographic segmentation to target parents of children under 12 years of age, with high income, living in coastal areas where children spend time in the water.

To segment a B2B market, we use 'firmographics', which are for businesses what demographics are for people. Firmographics include things like:

- Industry
- Location
- Company size
- Status/structure
- Performance
- Job function

The basic idea behind firmographics is that similar companies will face similar problems and therefore will have a similar level of need for your product or service. The more companies have in common, the more similar their needs will be.

Crawford Boots uses firmographics to target Occupational Health and Safety managers at large underground mining companies (500 or more employees), who can make purchasing decisions for their teams.

Psychographic Segmentation

Psychographic segmentation categorises audiences and customers by factors that relate to their personalities and characteristics, such as:

- Personality traits
- Values
- Attitudes
- Interests
- Lifestyle
- Motivations
- Priorities
- Subconscious and conscious beliefs
- Psychological influences

Psychographic segmentation factors are subjective and require research to uncover and understand. This makes them slightly more difficult to identify than demographics or firmographics.

In a B2C context for example, Minnow Designs may choose to focus on customers who value quality and fashion.

In the B2B context, psychographic factors can include aspects of company culture: a firm's values; whether or not it has a hierarchical decision-making structure; its policies around equal opportunity; and whether it is environmentally aware.

For instance, Crawford Boots may target companies which explicitly specify workplace safety as a company value.

Behavioural Segmentation

While demographic and psychographic segmentation focus on who a customer is, behavioural segmentation focuses on how the customer acts. It includes things like:

- Purchasing habits
- Spending habits
- User status
- Brand interactions

Behavioural segmentation requires you to know about your customer's actions. These activities may relate to how a customer interacts with your brand or to other activities that happen away from your brand.

In the B2C space, Minnow Designs may choose to target customers who play water sports frequently.

Crawford Boots, on the other hand, may focus on companies that have recently launched a workplace injury reduction campaign, or on OH&S managers who are assessed on their ability to reduce workplace injuries and increase productivity.

How do we use these segmentation parameters to divide an international market?

MARKET SEGMENTATION STEPS

- **Start with the data you already have.** If you have been in business for a while, you are already sitting on a goldmine of data. Start by analysing your past sales history – it's extremely likely that you will find similarities among your customers. These similarities will help you predict which types of clients are more likely to have an interest in your offer, and this approach works for both domestic and international markets.

  If you are targeting international markets, and do not yet have any international clients, look at who you have worked with at home as a starting point for understanding who you might target overseas.

- **Determine the parameters for your segmentation.** You can set your criteria any way you like: by geography, company size, industry sector, age, whatever is relevant for your client base. Using more criteria will help you to narrow the field, giving you a more targeted set of prospects. For example targeting 'all law firms specialising in family law, with 10-50 staff, in England' will give you a narrower, more specific range of prospects than 'all law firms in the United Kingdom'. The narrower your targeting, the more your prospects will have in common and the more likely they are to have similar needs.

- **Choose a tool to segment your list.** I recommend LinkedIn Sales Navigator, because it lets you access the data of millions of international firms and individuals quickly and easily. Data sources and tools like Dun & Bradstreet, experian, Data Axle Genie, and Crunchbase can also help you develop lists of ideal international candidates. If you prefer to go low-tech and you are not dealing with a large volume of prospects, an Excel spreadsheet will get you started.
- **Compile your prospect list into one place.** You can use an Excel spreadsheet, LinkedIn or your CRM.
- **Apply your parameters to your list.** Once you have chosen your segmentation criteria, apply them to your list to create targeted prospects – the most promising leads you can find.
- **Highlight your international prospects.** Pull out the international prospects that fit your criteria and put them into a new list of high-priority prospects.

Your Ideal International Client

Now let's talk about your ideal client. This is the person offshore who sees your product and says,

"Yes, this solves my problem – I'll buy it!"

Understanding your IIC is extremely important. If your solution and marketing are not aligned with what the IIC wants, and the problems they want you to solve, they will not buy from you. It is vital to have an exact target, so that prospects can find you and you can find them.

There are two common problems here. Some companies have only a vague idea of a fictional client who they want to work with. If (as is often the case) the client does not exist, selling to them is virtually impossible. Secondly, companies often define their ideal client too broadly, or assume that international clients want the same thing as clients at home, which is often not the case. In both instances, the underlying problem is lack of research.

To create solutions and marketing that reach your IIC and solve their problems, you must find out *what their problems really are*, not what you imagine them to be.

HOW DO WE ALIGN WHAT PEOPLE WANT AND WHAT WE ARE OFFERING?

A great way of aligning your offering with what clients want is to build an Ideal International Client profile, based on a single segment. This profile delves into the client's goals, challenges and desires, to help you understand what clients are trying to do, what problems they are facing and what outcomes they want.

Gathering the following information helps you to know what sorts of products and services you should offer your potential clients.

- **Goals:** what clients are trying to get done, in their work and in their lives
- **Challenges:** the problems and obstacles that they are facing as they try to achieve their goals
- **Desires:** what outcomes clients want to achieve, or the concrete benefits that they are seeking

Goals are the things that your clients are trying to get done in their work or their life. A client goal could be:

- The tasks they are trying to perform and complete at work
- The problems they are trying to solve at home
- Personal needs that they are trying to satisfy.

When you are thinking about goals, make sure that you take the client's perspective – what you think of as important might not be a goal for your client.

Challenges are anything that annoys your clients before, during and after they attempt to achieve a goal, or anything that prevents them from reaching their goal. Challenges can also be risks or potentially negative outcomes, related to not achieving a goal.

Desires are the outcomes and benefits that your customers want. Some of these things are required or expected by clients and some would surprise them. Desires can include functional utility, social gains, positive emotions, and cost savings.

Goals, challenges and desires can all vary in their importance, severity and relevance. While your clients may have a variety of goals, challenges and desires, and although individual customer preferences vary, it's very important to get a sense of which of these really matter the most to clients, so that you can make sure that the products you are putting into the market help them to achieve their most important goals, solve their most important challenges and fulfil their most relevant desires.

GO TO THE SOURCE

There are several ways that you can source the information for your ideal client profile, including:

- **Interviews.** Draw up a list of questions and call your clients and potential clients directly for their input. This is a great way to get a deep understanding of what people are looking for, but it takes a lot of time and effort.

- **Focus group**. This is a tactic used by big firms, and can yield deep insights into what clients are looking for and how they feel about products. The downside is that they are complex to coordinate and can be expensive to run.
- **Create surveys**. Survey clients using free tools like Survey Monkey. This method has the advantage of being quick and inexpensive. The downside is that response rates to surveys are usually very low and the quality of data is often lower, because the format is inflexible.
- **Run a poll on social media**. Like surveys, social media polls are a 'quick and dirty' way of getting feedback from prospects. They are quick and inexpensive, but do not provide nuanced data about clients' goals, challenges and desires.
- **Commission professional market research**. This can include interviews, surveys and focus groups. Professional research is more expensive than DIY research, but the advantage is that you can leave the hard work to experienced researchers who know how to find the data you need.

In the end, whichever method you choose, it all comes down to this: ask people what they are trying to do, what they struggle with and what they need.

DIG FOR CONCRETE INFORMATION

To clearly differentiate between your prospects' goals, challenges and desires, get people to describe them as concretely as possible.

For example, when a customer says, *"Waiting in line was a waste of time"* ask after how many minutes exactly it began to feel like a waste of time. That way, you can note, *"Wasting more than X minutes standing in line"*.

When you understand how clients measure the severity of inconvenience, you can design better ways to solve their problems.

As you go through this process, you will discover that what matters to your clients and potential clients overseas is often quite different to what matters to clients in your domestic market.

WHAT IF I DO NOT HAVE A LIST OF POTENTIAL INTERNATIONAL CLIENTS?

If you are starting cold, with no list of international prospects, an interim solution is to begin creating your ideal client profile with your best guess as to what is important to your future customers. The caveat is that you will need to test those assumptions to make sure they truly reflect priorities from the client's perspective, before you have invested a lot of time and money in a particular strategy.

If this seems like a daunting task, it could be time to commission some professional research.

CREATING AN IDEAL INTERNATIONAL CLIENT AVATAR

"You can't hit a target you have not set."

It is as true in international business as it is elsewhere, and that is why it's so important to have a clearly defined international client persona.

It is easier to spend time dreaming up avatars of people you would like to sell to, rather than doing the hard work to figure out who you have been selling to, are likely to be able to sell to and what they really want and expect from your product.

However, as I have alluded to several times in this chapter, an effective avatar must be based on real information – qualitative and quantitative – to be useful. A clearly defined customer avatar will help you:

- Deliver and develop better products and services because you are able to anticipate your market's needs, behaviours, and concerns.
- Determine what kinds of media your ideal client is consuming so you know where your business should be present and active (social media, digital media, print publications, television).
- Be more effective in your marketing and sales. Your marketing budget will go a lot further and generate more impact dollars when you know exactly who to target and how to reach them.

HOW DO I CREATE AN IDEAL INTERNATIONAL CLIENT AVATAR?

The best way to create your Ideal International Client Avatar is to combine the data sourced during the segmentation exercise around demographics, behaviour, psychography and geography, with the information gathered from clients and potential clients around their goals, challenges and desires. If you run your research in enough depth, these two sources will give you the information you need to build a nuanced picture of the person, or persons, you should be targeting.

What about a B2B client avatar?

In the B2C space, targeting your product is all about facilitating ease: what problem is your buyer facing that could be fixed by your product or service? How can you ease their mind or bring overall ease to their lives? The good news is that translating the buyer persona to the B2B world is also fairly easy to do.

In the B2B world, an effective client avatar maps two things:

- The corporate context
- The need for decision makers and influencers to more effectively navigate that context.

For B2B companies, the buyer's context is the company. By looking at your most profitable and engaged customers, you will quickly see patterns that will help you understand the context.

It is also worth expanding your universe to look at customers that surprised you (i.e. responded well to your product or got a lot of value from it) and your aspirational customers (i.e., your dream client) when developing data files. What you want to understand about them is:

- Basic demographics – industry, size, who they serve, number of employees, revenues, footprint, etc.
- Biggest objectives as a firm for the year ahead
- Biggest obstacles for them as a firm for the year ahead

- Industry dynamics – the bigger context around your customer's business
- What changes the pain points that you want to alleviate.

I want to focus on the idea of change for a minute. It is central to understanding the B2B buyer. Businesses rarely innovate for innovation's sake. The decision to buy a new accounting system is driven by something such as growth in revenues that an old system cannot keep up with; a lack of features that are adequate to the demands of public reporting prior to an IPO; or changes in technology that allow more flexible mobile reporting.

Whatever the situation is, something has happened that makes this urgent or important enough to focus resources on now.

Here are some questions that you can ask to better understand what is changing for your B2B client:

- What is important to them and what is driving the change?
- What is impeding or speeding their need to change?
- How do they go about change?
- What do they need to know to embrace change?
- Who do they turn to for advice or information?
- What is the value they visualise once they make a decision?
- Who do they have to sell the change to in order to achieve it?
- What could cause the need for this change to lose priority?

The second area that you need to profile encompasses your decision makers and influencers. In effect, this change in the bigger corporate context has created a change for your buyer's job.

You must understand that ripple effect and capture that critical data in your profile. Answering this question will win you sales.

"How does this corporate change affect your buyer?"

At the decision maker and influencer level, you need to understand who is involved and be able to answer the following:

- What is their job title and core responsibilities?
- Who evaluates their performance?
- What aspect of their performance evaluation can your product assist, such as increasing efficiencies or cutting costs?
- What is at risk if they make a bad decision regarding this purchase?
- Who else in the organisation will they impact with their decision?
- How has the bigger company change or pressure impacted them personally?

It is less important that your B2B buyer in Singapore is Jenny, a 35-year-old office manager who manages two administrative assistants. It is more important to know that Jenny needs to find a way to report her team's productivity to her boss, who sees administrative support as a cost centre and is under increasing pressure to manage his P&L.

Once you have created an avatar for your Ideal International Client or clients, you will be in a strong position to map their goals, challenges and desires against your offering. That is the subject of our next chapter.

CHAPTER 6

MAKING SURE YOUR PRODUCT WILL SELL – BEFORE YOU START SELLING

CHAPTER 6

MAKING SURE YOUR PRODUCT WILL SELL – BEFORE YOU START SELLING

When it comes to selling internationally, mistakes are often made around the fit between the product and market. It is easy to understand how it happens. When companies are intimately acquainted with the desires and expectations of customers at home, and have been meeting those to a high standard for a long time, they can get complacent. When the time comes to expand to new markets overseas, leaders tend to think,

"We know people buy our product and we know what works best for our clients. We'll replicate what we've done at home overseas and everything will be fine."

But this is not the case, as a bunch of companies (including large ones) have learned the hard way.

The initial failure of Starbucks in Australia is a great example.[12] Starbuckshas coffee shops all over the world. There are more than 28,000 locations and 76 markets, from Shanghai to Guantanamo Bay. But when Starbucks launched in Australia, it discovered that 'the land down under' was one of the toughest markets in the world to break into.

The company opened its first Australian shop in Sydney in July 2000 and expanded rapidly.

Because of its success elsewhere, Starbucks believed that it could 'copy and paste' its business model to Australia without customisation. Starbucks did not realise that, when it comes to coffee, Australians are spoiled for choice. They have been immersed in the nuances of cafe culture since the mid-1900s, when Italian and Greek immigrants began arriving in droves, bringing espresso coffee with them.

Cafes in Australia were born out of the Italian culture of meeting a friend and knowing your local barista. The cafe was a local meeting place where everyone knew each other and coffee was a part of that experience. By the 1980s, Australians were fully engulfed in cafe culture and had also grown accustomed to specialty menu items like a flat white or an Australian macchiato.

Starbucks introduced a very different, American-style coffee culture which focused primarily on coffee as a product. It had a basic menu and offered a range of sugary drinks, which most Australians did not like. Starbucks also charged more than local cafes. Australians responded by opting to pay less money for coffee they liked better, from a local barista they trusted.

By 2008, there were 87 Starbucks stores across the continent. The company had accumulated losses of more than $105 million and borrowed an eye-watering $54 million from its parent company in the US. Starbucks Australia announced it was shutting down 61 stores, two thirds of its Australian business.

Starbucks has since adapted its strategy and re-engaged with the Australian market. However, its story confirms that even if you have a wildly successful brand at home, it will not necessarily work overseas. This is because how customers perceive and engage with a brand differs from country to country.

There are several indicators that signal a company has not nailed its international product-market fit. These include launching in a new market without:

- A clear value proposition for *that specific country*
- Insight into how well a product meets the customers' desires *in that market*
- Confirmation that the company can make sales *in that market.*

If you start selling internationally without this knowledge, there's a real risk that your sales results will not match your revenue forecasts. The solution?

- Get clear on the value proposition for your ideal client in the international market you are targeting.
- Make sure that your offering solves a problem for that particular client.
- Provide evidence that clients in your target market will pay what you are asking.

Getting clear on your value proposition

The easiest way to get clear on your value proposition for a particular client in a particular segment is to create a ***Value Map***, which describes the features of an offering in your business model, in a structured way.

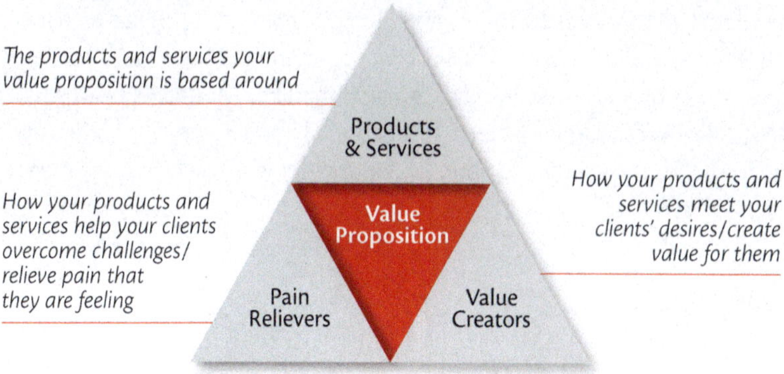

The Value Map

A Value Map breaks a value proposition down into three parts.

PRODUCTS AND SERVICES

Product and services is the list of what you offer – think of it as all the products that your customer can see in your 'shop window' – anything they can buy from you. This bundle of products and services helps your clients get things done or helps them satisfy basic needs.

Your value proposition could be made up of different types of products and services including:

- **Physical/tangible** – e.g. manufactured products, food, clothes, phones
- **Intangible** – products such as copyrights, professional services, after-sales service
- **Digital** – products such as music downloads or online recommendations
- **Financial** – insurance, foreign exchange, financing a purchase, investment funds.

It is important to remember that no matter how great your offering is, products and services by themselves do not create value. Value is created only in relationship to a specific customer segment and the goals, challenges and desires of the people in that segment. That is why not all products and services have the same relevance to all your customers and why some parts of your offer are essential to your value proposition, while others are merely nice to have.

PAIN RELIEVERS

Pain relievers describe how your products and services address your clients' challenges. They explicitly outline how your offering eliminates or reduces some of the things that annoy your customers before, during or after they try to accomplish a goal, or anything that prevents them from accomplishing the goal.

Great value propositions focus on challenges that matter to your customers, in particular extreme challenges. You do not need to come up with a pain reliever for every challenge that your client is facing, you just need to overcome a few extreme challenges very well.

Strong value propositions also recognise that a pain reliever can be more or less relevant to a client, depending on their circumstances.

For example, imagine you sell a pocket-sized portable speaker with Bluetooth capability, a 10-hour battery life and a waterproof case. The speaker itself relieves the pain of picnics and beach visits without hi-fidelity music for consumers all over the world. The waterproof case also relieves the pain of having your speaker ruined by a sudden downpour during a picnic. However, the waterproof case relieves a pain which is far more real for consumers in rainy Britain than for consumers in sunny California.

As you create your Value Map, make sure that you are clear about which pain relievers are essential for your international customers, and which ones are just nice to have. Essential pain relievers fix extreme challenges, often in a radical way, and create a lot of value. Nice to have pain relievers fix less significant problems and tend to be features which the product could still operate well without.

VALUE CREATORS

A Value Map also includes value creators: ways in which your products and services create value for clients by helping them attain their desires. Value creators explicitly outline how you will produce the outcomes and benefits that your client expects, desires or would be surprised by.

As with pain relievers, value creators do not need to meet all your clients' desires. Focus on those that are most relevant to your clients and on areas where your offer can really make a difference.

Pain relievers and value creators create value for the client in different ways. The difference is that pain relievers specifically address challenges in the client profile, while value creators specifically address clients' goals (things that they are trying to get done by using your product).

It is fine if aspects of your product address goals and challenges at the same time. The real objective is to make it very clear that your products and services create value for your customers, in ways that they care about.

Finding 'fit'

You achieve 'fit' when clients get excited about your value proposition, which happens when you address important goals, overcome challenges and fulfil desires that clients care about.

In an international context, 'fit' happens in three stages:

- You identify the goals, challenges and desires of potential clients overseas that you believe you can address with your value proposition
- Clients react positively to your value proposition and it starts to get traction in the new market
- You find a business model and delivery channels in the new country that are scalable and profitable.

To find out whether your product fits with what your Ideal International Client is looking for:

- Compare your Ideal International Client profile and Value Map
- Go through the Pain Relievers and Value Creators one by one, and check to see whether they fit a client, goal, challenge or desire
- If a Pain Reliever or Value Creator does not fit anything, it may not be creating value for clients
- Ask yourself how well your value proposition really fits your customer? Are there things that you might need to change?

Clients expect and desire a lot from products and services, but they also know they cannot have it all. The key is to focus on the things that matter most to clients and how you can address them.

Once you understand your client's preferences, you will be able to work out whether your product, as it stands, will do the trick, or whether you will need to modify it in some way. It will also help you to understand whether you can sell your product or service at a price that makes sense.

WILL THEY PAY?

Another mistake that I see people making as they try to break into a new international market is not knowing before they start whether clients in that market are willing to pay what they are asking.

The customer's willingness to pay should be at the core of your international strategy, because if something costs a lot to make and distribute but no-one wants to buy it, you will end up losing a lot of time and money. Ironically, most companies postpone marketing and pricing decisions to the very end, when they have already developed their products. They begin the long and costly journey of product development hoping they will make money on their innovations, but not knowing if they will. The same goes for companies taking existing products to new countries – knowing whether your international customers will pay is often left until the last moment, or overlooked altogether, sometimes with disastrous results.

Some years ago, a colleague of mine, Peter, owned a company that sold dried Australian fruit and nuts. It expanded around the world, including to China and the United States, where it had customers including giants like Walmart. Peter's dream was to see his products on the shelves of UK supermarket chain Sainsbury's and he made plans to launch his product there. He says:

> *"Selling in the UK was something I'd always wanted to do, but I didn't look at pricing at the very start of the process. Luckily before we got as far as beginning to sell, I made a visit to the UK, and as I stood in Sainsbury's looking at similar products, I realised that my plan wasn't going to work. The prices of competitor products were much lower than our proposed prices and there was just no way we could compete. It was a bit disappointing, but I'm glad I found out the truth about what UK consumers would pay before I'd made a big investment of time and money, pursuing the wrong strategy."*

Most companies develop an offer for an international market like this: they design, then build, then market and price. I suggest you do the opposite. I believe you should market and price, then design, then build. In other words, design your offering around what people are willing to pay. This is especially relevant if you are going into a country where you are competing with a range of other companies, selling products that solve the same or similar problems.

How do you do that?

THE 'WILLINGNESS TO PAY' CONVERSATION

Whether you are launching an existing product into an overseas market or designing something new for one, a key step you can take is to have the 'willingness to pay' conversation early.

Essentially, this means talking to potential customers about your product or service, finding out which parts of the offering are most valuable for them and getting their feedback on the pricing you have in mind. If you do not do this exercise early on, you lose the opportunity to prioritise the products that you choose to sell to the new market or the product features that you develop especially for that market. Most importantly, you will not know whether your potential clients will pay *before* you make a big investment in a certain strategy.

I will close this chapter with a story about Gillette, a company that does international product-market fit and pricing better than most.

In 2009, Gillette razor brands accounted for more than 60% of razor and blade sales in the US and about 70% of the world's total razor and blade sales. But in India, a market with the potential to be four times bigger than America's for shaving products, the company had just a 22% market share, because its products were expensive for the Indian market.

To increase market share in India, the company realised that it had to target the lower-to-middle income segment of the population. To do this, Gillette decided to create a new product for Indian men, but before they did so, they spent a lot of time interviewing people in India and other emerging markets. Gillette observed potential clients at home and on shopping trips to understand what features razors *had to have*, and which features were *nice to have*.

Gillette designed and priced a new razor, the Guard®, on the basis of its research. The Guard razor has a single blade, a hollow handle, and cost just 34cents,[13] a fraction of the cost of a premium product. The results were swift and stunning. By 2012, the Guard had captured 60% of the razor category in India, tripling Gillette's market share there.

As the Gillette story shows, taking the time to ensure a 'fit' between your Ideal International Client and your product has the potential to dramatically improve your results in international markets.

CHAPTER 7

‘IT’S A RED OCEAN OUT THERE...’

CHAPTER 7

'IT'S A RED OCEAN OUT THERE...' SUSSING OUT THE COMPETITION

Because 'going global' is such an involved process, doing competitor analysis is often overlooked. Myths abound in this space. CEOs say things like,

"We're just going to focus on what we do and not get hung up on the competition."

Or *"We're just a small company, we don't need to do competitor analysis, that's for the big guys."*

Or, best of all, *"We don't have any competitors, no-one else makes this product!"*

Let's get real here. All businesses face competition. Even if you are the only pub in town you must compete with other businesses where your customers will spend their money to be entertained – cinemas, restaurants, and the racetrack.

And, because people are increasingly searching for and buying goods and services online, you are no longer just competing with your immediate neighbours in your target geography. You may very well find yourself competing with businesses from other countries too.

Your competitor could be:

- A new business offering a substitute or similar product that makes your own redundant
- Another product or service that is being developed and which you ought to be selling or looking to license before somebody else takes it up.

Even if you have a product or service which is a one-of-a-kind, it will still have competition, it just will not be direct competition.

Understanding your competition is important. If you do not know who your competitors are, or how they compare to you, you will not be across the threats they pose, nor have a strategy for dealing with them.

Three types of competitors

At the macro level, there are only three types of competitors that matter. These competitors apply across all industries and business types.

DIRECT COMPETITORS

A direct competitor is probably what most commonly comes to mind when you think of the word 'competition'.

This is someone who offers the same products as you, with the same end game. They make money from the same thing you do.

Direct competitors are similar to you in multiple aspects of a product or service offering. They may or may not compete with all the same services, the delivery might be different, or they may have a different marketing strategy. Maybe you sell red apples and they sell green. You market the sweetness of your apples, your competitor highlights the texture of theirs, but you are targeting the same customers.

In direct competition the most common bases for companies to compete are geography covered and price given to customers. Relationship management plays a major role in wooing customers and taking away market share from direct competitors. If a customer gets excellent service from your organisation, he or she is unlikely to move to a competitor.

INDIRECT COMPETITORS

Indirect competitors offer the same stuff but have a different goal. They do not drive revenue the same way. For example, you may sell an online game for a fee while another company provides a similar game free, as part of its marketing. The free product will compete with your paid product for people's attention.

REPLACEMENT COMPETITORS

A replacement competitor offers consumers an alternative option to consume with the resources they may have spent on your product.

For example, if you operate a cinema, a replacement competitor is anything your would-be customer chooses to do for entertainment instead of going to the cinema. They may watch a movie at home. They may read a book, go to a restaurant or visit friends – all of these are replacements for spending time being entertained in our cinema.

Replacement competitors are the most challenging competitors to identify. The best way to find them is to interview customers, eavesdrop on their social media conversations and understand macro trends, to understand the consumption choices they make.

Knowing your competitors

Do you already know who your competitors in your target international market are? If you do not, you will need to do some digging to identify them.

You can get clues about competitors from:

- Advertising
- Press reports
- Exhibitions and trade fairs
- Questionnaires
- Searching online for similar products or services

- Information provided by customers
- Flyers and marketing literature that have been sent to you – quite common if you are on a purchased marketing list
- Searching for existing patented products similar to yours
- Chambers of commerce.

Building up the picture

Once you have worked out who your competitors are, your next job is to find out about them – to build up a detailed picture to use to create a competitor analysis. This can be the hard part. While you can always approach your competitors directly, they may or may not be willing to tell you what you need to know to put together your competitor analysis.

You need to know:

- What markets or market segments your competitors serve
- What benefits your competitors offer
- Why customers buy from them
- As much as possible about their products and/or services, pricing, and promotion, including:
    - The products or services they provide
    - How they market to customers
    - The prices they charge
    - How they distribute and deliver
- The devices they employ to enhance customer loyalty
- Any back-up service they offer
- Their brand and design values
- Whether they innovate – business methods as well as products
- Their staff numbers and the calibre of staff they attract
- How they use IT – are they technology-aware? Do they offer a website? Do they communicate by email or other digital channels?
- Who owns the business and what sort of person they are
- What the annual report tells you – if it is a public company

- Their media activities – check their website as well as local newspapers, radio, television and any outdoor advertising.

You should also find out as much as possible about your competitors' customers, such as:

- Who they are
- What products or services they buy from your competitors
- What they see as your competitors' strengths and weaknesses
- Whether there are any long-standing customers
- If they have recently increased.

Try to go beyond what is happening now by investigating your competitors' business strategy, for example:

- What types of customers are they targeting?
- What new products are they developing?
- What financial resources do they have?

So, how do you build that picture?

READ ABOUT YOUR COMPETITORS

Look for articles or ads in the trade press or mainstream publications. Read their marketing literature. Check their entries in directories. If they are an online business, ask for a trial of their service. Are they getting more publicity than you, perhaps through networking or sponsoring events? If your competitor is a public company, read a copy of their annual report.

GO TO EXHIBITIONS

At exhibitions and trade fairs check which of your competitors are also exhibiting. Look at their stands and promotional activities. Note how busy they are and who visits them.

GO ONLINE

Look at your competitors' websites. Find out how they compare to yours. Check any interactive parts of the site to see if you could make your own website do it better. Is the information free of charge? Is it easy to find?

Business websites often give away much more information than businesses have traditionally revealed – from the history of the company to biographies of the staff.

Use a search engine to track down similar products. Find out who else offers them and how they go about it.

Websites can give you good tips on what businesses around the globe are doing in your industry sector.

SPEAK TO YOUR COMPETITORS

Phone them to ask for a copy of their brochure or get one of your staff or a friend to drop by and pick up their marketing literature.

You could ask for a price list or enquire what an off-the-shelf item might cost and if there is a discount for volume. This will give you an idea at which point a competitor will discount and at what volume.

Phone and face-to-face contacts will also give you an idea of the style of the company, the quality of their literature and the initial impressions they make on customers.

It is also likely you will meet competitors at social and business events. Talk to them. Be friendly – they are competitors not enemies, and you may end up collaborating in future, and friendliness will get you more information.

LISTEN TO YOUR CUSTOMERS AND SUPPLIERS

Make the most of contacts with your customers. Do not just ask how well you are performing – ask which of your competitors they buy from and how you compare.

Use meetings with your suppliers to ask what their other customers are doing. They may not tell you everything you want to know, but it is a useful start.

Use your judgement with any information they volunteer. For instance, when customers say your prices are higher than the competition they may just be trying to negotiate a better deal.

Analyse your competitors

Once you have collected information about the competitors that are present in your target market, study the insights that you have generated about each of them and ask:

"How are we going to compete with our competitors?"

One of the keys to competing successfully, at home and abroad (especially for small businesses), is to identify a market niche where you can capture a specific target market whose needs are not being met.

Good questions to ask here include:

- Is there a particular segment of the market that your competition has overlooked?
- Is there a service that customers or clients want that your competitor does not supply?

The goal of your competitor analysis is to identify and expand upon your competitive advantage – the benefits that your business can offer the customer or client that your competition cannot or will not supply.

Create your competitor analysis

If you want to get really serious and take it a step further, you can formalise your digging and thinking into a competitor analysis. This is a document that contains the following sections.

- **The competitive environment.** This section outlines the competitive environment, identifies who your competitors are, how much of the market they control and any other relevant details about the competition.
- **Competitors' products/services.** Outline your competitors' products and services here. Think specifically in terms of the features, value provided to customers and how exactly they are being sold. Do not forget to include details on how your competitors are marketing and distributing their products. Include information on product quality and find out how they are staffed and are operating (when you can).
- **Competitors' strengths and weaknesses.** Be objective as you assess the strengths/weaknesses of your competition. A competitive analysis is useless if you allow your own belief in your products to cloud reality. Think about their products as if you actually work for the competitor, and discover what makes them so great. Is it the quality or are they more user-friendly? If they are growing rapidly, is there a particular product or service that is key to their growth?
- **Competitors' strategies.** Use the 'strategies' section of your analysis to paint a picture of how your competitors are going about building and maintaining their competitive position.
- **Market overview.** Give an overview of the market. Study the trends and figure out what the actual customers for your products are looking for. If the demand is growing there are probably going to be plenty of customers around. On the flip side, a flat or declining market will see fierce competition. This is not a good market to be in, as everyone scrambles to win (or maintain) market share. Focus on any niches that might be developing, and make sure you are targeting what the customers actually want. By the time you get to this stage of the analysis you are going to have more than enough information to measure and determine a future outlook from the trends.

- **How we will compete.** Use the final paragraphs to explain your competitive advantage, explaining why and how your company will be able to compete with these competitors and establish yourself as a successful business in your new international market.

Once you have completed this process, you will be ready to face your competitors, anywhere.

CHAPTER 8 BRIDGING THE CULTURAL DIVIDE

CHAPTER 8

BRIDGING THE CULTURAL DIVIDE

I know from experience that one of the key challenges that companies – small and large – face when it comes to international expansion is bridging the cultural divide. Adapting to the culture of a new market is not just about switching up your packaging or rebranding your company's name so that it works in that country, although these things are important pieces of the puzzle. Cultural difference begins with how a place looks or feels, what people eat and wear and how they speak. But it goes much deeper than that, and that is where the complexity comes in. Here are some of the key problems that pop up frequently.

- **You do not know what you do not know.** Arriving in a new country or dealing with a new culture for the first time usually feels very different to what you are used to, but it can be hard to put your finger on exactly what is different (apart from very obvious things) and why. This can cause confusion and make your initial engagement with the new setting difficult.
- **'Copy and paste'**. I have met a lot of people who are successful in one country who believe that they can just deploy the same strategies that they use to build relationships and negotiate business at home in a new market. It almost never works.

- **No tools.** Finally, the majority of people do not have the tools and know-how to work in a cross-cultural business setting.

These challenges often lead to friction in business relationships, and potential clients and partners reacting in unexpected or unwelcome ways. As a result, international businesses and global partnerships do not get off the ground because the people trying to create them are not equipped to work cross-culturally.

The first step is to get your assumptions and expectations straight when it comes to working internationally.

Assume that cultural differences exist

Business owners often do not appreciate just *how* different the culture of a new market is before they get started.

This is normal.

If you have always lived and worked in your own country, you will probably be unaware of your own culture and the way it has shaped you. Like the air you breathe, it is a key part of life, but you cannot see, smell, taste, touch or hear it – it's just there.

You may also be unaware of how differently people in other cultures have been shaped by their own culture. The result? You are unprepared for the extent of the cultural differences that you will face as you take your business overseas.

This can be the case even when you are expanding to another country which is culturally similar to your own. People from the West expect that other Western cultures will be more or less the same, but it's not always the case. When I was a university student, I had to spend a year abroad as part of my degree. I was supposed to be heading to Japan, as Japanese was a language I had studied before. But instead, I opted to spend the year in France, because I spoke French reasonably well and I assumed that France would be an easy place to live. I could not have been more wrong. I found myself catapulted into a French university town in the middle of winter. It was cold, it was grey and everyone had already made friends in the first term (which started in autumn). I partially understood the language, but I struggled to understand the social cues and my first six months in France were tough.

I remember being invited to lunch at the home of a friend of a friend in Paris, a couple of months after I arrived. I had agreed to be there by midday, but got lost in the capital's winding streets and got to lunch about 40 minutes late – not a good way to make a strong first impression. I turned up bedraggled, embarrassed and anxious that everyone seemed put out. It was only years later that I realised that because many Parisians do not eat breakfast at the weekend (to keep space for lunch), and people are very hungry by midday, Sunday lunch tends to start on the dot and being late for it is considered a cardinal sin. Over my time in France, I worked out how to fit in, but it was a difficult introduction to a culture that I had assumed would be easy.

Five years later when I moved to Egypt, I faced a whole bunch of cultural challenges that were far more extreme than just knowing what the rules around lunch were.

In Egypt, everything was different. Time worked backwards to how it had in France – if I hosted a dinner party, friends would turn up two or more hours later than I had invited them, and seemed to think it was normal. Taxis would try to charge me multiple times the real fare as I was conspicuously un-Egyptian (and taxis had no meters). I was considered strange because I was single and female and lived alone rather than with my family. I once offended an Egyptian friend because I did not stay by his bed when he was ill. I assumed he would want peace and quiet to sleep while he was sick and he assumed that I did not care about him because I left him alone. It was a classic case of cultural miscommunication.

I could fill an entire book with stories about the cultural differences that I encountered in Europe, the Middle East, the United States and Asia, but the point that I want to make is this:

> ***"It is better to begin by assuming that cultural differences will exist when you do business internationally, and acknowledge that it is your job to uncover them."***

Appreciate that each market will need a different cultural approach

Because each country has its own culture, it's important to appreciate that each market will need a slightly different cultural approach, and it might need to be a little different, or very different, from your home culture.

When companies are expanding to another country which seems culturally similar, they do all sorts of other preparation – create a great pitch deck, work out pricing, investigate logistics – but they do not do anything about culture because they figure that if they can communicate with their counterparts in the same language then everything will be ok. They make no effort to understand cultural differences and the impact that these could have on how successful they are in the new place.

I have a colleague who experienced first-hand that what works in China will not work in Japan. Quinn had worked in China setting up subsidiaries for a large international company. He had spent two years there, learning how to do things, and as he says,

"Making heaps of mistakes."

Just as he had mastered working in China, he was transferred to Japan, to do a similar job, because his company assumed he had 'Asia skills'. Quinn tried to take what he had learned in China to Japan but found that it did not work at all, because the business culture was different.

Once you recognise that you need to get prepared for cultural differences in the same way that you prepare for every other part of your international business strategy, you can get to work.

What is culture?

As I mentioned above, culture has visible and invisible layers. The visible aspects of culture include the way people dress, their behaviour (verbal and non-verbal language), food, buildings, customs and traditions. The less visible aspects of culture include values, beliefs, norms, perceptions and philosophies, and these intangible aspects of culture are the most important

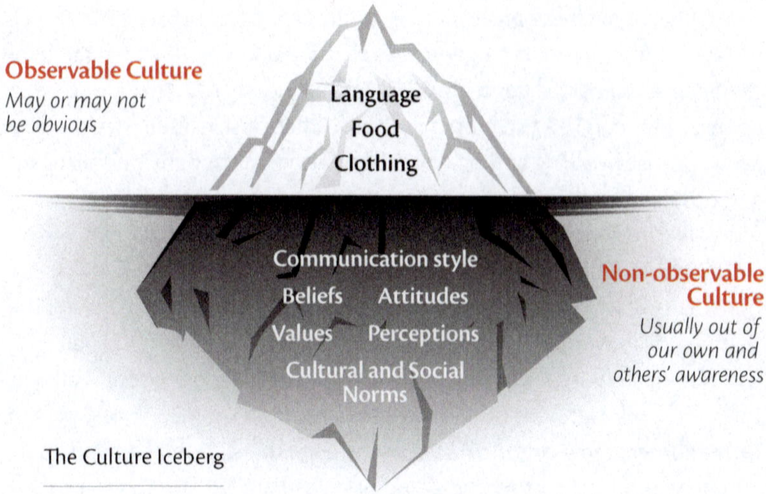

The Culture Iceberg

because they influence our perceptions and the way we think and act. Moreover, because we have a natural tendency to revert to our cultural roots, how we behave and make decisions are all affected by cultural values, even if we are not aware of it. For instance, it was my Australian cultural background that made me conclude that leaving a sick friend to sleep was a kind thing to do, while my friend's Egyptian cultural background led him to see the same behaviour as uncaring. At the time, neither of us was aware of how significantly culture fed into this episode.

The huge impact that culture has on how we think and act means that it's very important to understand other cultures if we want to do business in culturally diverse settings. In the remainder of this chapter, I want to touch on some of the key topics and themes that you should be aware of as you start working overseas. I will also make some suggestions about things that you can do to prepare for cross-cultural interactions.

CHALLENGE STEREOTYPES

Challenging the stereotypes that you have about other cultures is a good place to start. Stereotypes are oversimplified ideas about certain groups of people which can affect our own attitudes and expectations as we communicate with people from that group. Stereotypes can be positive or negative and by stereotyping we infer that a person has a whole range of characteristics and abilities that we assume all members of that group have. For example, common stereotypes about Americans include that they are generous, hardworking and optimistic, but also that they are loud, arrogant and obsessed with guns.

Or, when doing business in Europe we might expect our Italian counterparts to be late for a meeting whereas a Swiss would always be punctual and well organised. However, it would be inappropriate to assume that no Italian would ever be on time and no Swiss would ever be late.

Using stereotypes is a way in which we simplify our social world, as they reduce the amount of thinking required when we meet a new person or encounter a new culture. A stereotype gives the illusion of a predictable pattern we can learn, providing a kind of boilerplate for how to react to any given cross-cultural situation. The problem is that while they can help us get a very general idea about a culture, stereotypes are general, not accurate, and individual people often do not conform to stereotypes. That is why cross-cultural stereotypes need to be treated carefully – they can have a negative impact on our thinking and our capacity to perceive things with discernment.

When you are doing business internationally, get ready to challenge the initial stereotypes that you have about the people in your new target market.

DIFFERENT LENS

Our starting point to unpacking and understanding different cultures is that a lot of what we call culture is perspective. Each of us has different perspectives on the world that are shaped by the circumstances we grew up in; our education and the norms that our family and society taught us. Geert Hofstede, a famous Dutch sociologist calls culture 'the software of the mind'. It's how we are programmed.

The idea that culture is closely tied to perspective can be hard to get your head around if you have always lived in one culture, because it feels like the way you see the world is the 'right' way.

Here is the thing, though: someone who has also grown up in one culture (that is entirely different to your culture) can also have a single view on the world that they feel is the 'right' one. And they will be just as certain about that as you are.

TIP Understand that people see the world through different lenses, and factor that into how you act or react to circumstances.

PAY ATTENTION TO HIERARCHY AND STATUS

In what are known as 'high power distance' societies, which include countries like China and Japan, status and hierarchy matter. Respect for, and deference to, superiors is very important, in all areas of life. For example, Richard Lewis, author of *When Cultures Collide: Leading Across Cultures* says of Malaysia (which has a power distance score of 100/100):

> *"Status is inherited, not earned, and is confirmed by demonstrating leadership and a caring attitude. Malays feel comfortable in a hierarchical structure in which they have a definite role."*

In these kinds of cultures, people at the top of the hierarchy enjoy privileges which are not available to those lower down the hierarchy. For example, when I lived in the UAE, I had to visit my bank from time to time. When I did, it was normal for me to be escorted to the front of the queue, ahead of all the Arab and Filipino customers who had been patiently waiting their turn. That was because I was female, white and a diplomat. Coming from a very egalitarian culture where you wait your turn in the queue no matter who you are, this made me uncomfortable. I also did not like it when I was talking to the bank teller and an Emirati man in traditional dress elbowed me out of the way and began loudly voicing his request. To everyone else in the bank, this kind of behaviour appeared unremarkable because, as an Emirati man, he held a higher rank than I did. But I really minded it. That is probably because in 'low power distance' cultures like Holland, Australia and New Zealand, much less emphasis is placed on hierarchy and there is a general expectation that society will work democratically.

Within Australian companies for example, flat structures are common and there is an understanding that everyone is inherently equal. Where they exist, hierarchies are often established merely for convenience. Superiors are usually accessible and managers rely on individual employees and teams for their expertise. Both managers and employees share information frequently and expect to be consulted. Communication between different levels of an organisation is informal, direct and participative. People call each other by their first names. This is quite different to how things work in a Japanese or Emirati company where titles are important and communication is formal. In high power distance cultures, the person of higher status usually gets to speak first, set the agenda and have the final say. Conversely, in low power distance countries, anyone can speak up if they have a valid point to make and decisions are often made collectively.

One of the most important differences between high and low power distance cultures is whether or not a subordinate is allowed to directly confront their boss about an issue. This includes asking questions. In low power distance countries, employees are expected to ask questions and to tell their superiors when something does not seem to be correct. In a high power distance culture, employees do not ask questions, and they do not point out obvious errors that a superior has made. You can imagine the kinds of challenges that can crop up when people from low and high power distance societies begin working together without an awareness of these differences.

As you do business in a high power distance culture, you may also find that you are not necessarily talking with the final decision-maker and you may need to allow greater time for your contact to get the necessary approvals within the organisation to move forward than you would at home. This is often frustrating for businesspeople from low power distance cultures, as they struggle to understand why business moves at what appears to be a glacial pace.

Conversely, if you are from a high power distance culture, your counterpart may be in a position to make decisions quickly and independently, and your deal may move forward faster than you were expecting.

RULES VS RELATIONSHIPS

Cultures can also be categorised as either relationship-based or rule-based. While rule-based cultures and relationship-based cultures both have rules, the differences between them have significant implications for how business is done.

In a relationship-based culture, relationships are a key driver of behaviour and authority figures – parents, bosses, elder siblings or even departed ancestors – do the regulating. Bad behaviour is deterred by shame, loss of face, punishment, or ostracism. Because the authority figures are close at hand and form an integral part of the social environment, everyone knows what appropriate behaviour looks like and there is no need to spell it out explicitly.

Behaviour in rule-based cultures, on the other hand, is based on respect for rules. People respect and obey the rules for their own sake, not because someone in a position of authority made a rule.

The dichotomy between rules- and relationship-based culture is particularly apparent if you are a Westerner doing business in the Gulf States. There, it is common to hear people talking about using '*wasta*' – which translates as 'influence' or 'connections' – to resolve a conflict or get things done. Using *wasta* usually means bypassing official channels or bending the rules to get a faster or more favourable result. In fact, if you do not have *wasta*, getting anything done quickly in these countries can be a struggle. It is the normal and preferred way of doing business in the Middle East. To rule-obsessed Westerners though, it reeks of nepotism, cutting corners and doing back-room deals, all of which are frowned on in Western culture. Australians, Americans and Brits feel irritated by the idea of someone getting a great outcome specifically because they *did not* play by the rules or do things 'the official way'.

Or, consider how contracts work in a country like China. Whereas something as simple as hiring a car in Europe requires you to sign a five-page contract, dealing with every possible contingency, it is possible to begin a major commercial deal in China on a handshake (although as a rule-obsessed Western lawyer, I personally do not recommend it). Where there is a written contract in China, it may be more of a memorandum of understanding than a binding legal document.[14] Because the terms are vague, there is room for adjustment as the situation evolves. As for compliance, the parties are more likely to rely on a relationship of trust than a legal system.

This kind of fluidity makes rules-based people uneasy, but for a Chinese person it makes sense. In a Confucian culture, doing business is primarily about developing personal relationships – not just doing a transaction. These can be based on family or clan connections, or on relationships of mutual obligation, '*guanxi*', which also translates as 'connection'. Business plans develop along with the relationship rather than through formal documents, and while businesspeople draw up contracts to please their Western counterparts, stories abound about the Chinese side wanting to alter the terms the day after the document is signed. While this is shocking for the Westerner who thinks,

"I cannot believe they want to start moving the goalposts already!"

the Chinese thinking is,

"Why enslave oneself to a piece of paper, when the world constantly changes?"

THE GROUP OR THE INDIVIDUAL?

Individualism and collectivism describe the degree of interdependence among the members of a society. In individualistic societies the ties between individuals are loose: everyone is expected to look after himself or herself and his or her immediate family. In collective societies people are integrated into strong, cohesive in-groups from birth onward. Through a person's lifetime, the group protects them in exchange for unquestioning loyalty. Here is an example of how these differences can play out in an international business context.

Imagine that Paul is an American visiting his company's Japanese partner in Tokyo for the first time. He has been talking with his counterpart, Taro, at least once a week for the last six months. Paul thinks that Taro has done a great job supporting the company's Japanese clients, and he wants to make sure Taro gets the recognition he deserves.

At the beginning of the visit, Paul meets with the partner's key staff, including Taro. He wants to show his appreciation and build some goodwill, so he praises Taro's dedication and skills in front of his peers. The mood in the room suddenly shifts and Taro seems visibly embarrassed. Everyone else looks uncomfortable too. What just happened?

As an American, Paul comes from a business culture where individual achievement is highly prized. What he does not realise is that the majority of business cultures around the world place a higher value on group membership and dynamics and that Japan is one of the most collectivist societies in the world. By singling out a group member, Paul made Taro lose face in front of his team and the team shared his embarrassment. This is true even though Paul was recognising Taro for positive reasons. The Japanese expression for this is:

"The nail that sticks up gets hammered down."

Much of the world's population lives and works in cultures that are more collectivist than individualistic. As a Westerner working internationally, how can you adjust to work effectively with collectivist mindsets?

For starters, the next time you find yourself in conversation with a key contact from Asia, the Middle East, Latin America or Africa, be conscious of how much time you spend talking about individuals versus the group. While it makes sense to inquire after your contact's health, it is also smart to ask how their team is doing. If you are meeting with someone from a culture that co-mingles work and private life, inquire about the health and well-being of their family as well. As you move forward in conversation, keep in mind the impact of potential decisions on other group members both in your organisation and your counterpart's.

COMMUNICATION STYLES

In Anglo-Saxon cultures – the United States, United Kingdom, Canada, Australia and New Zealand – we are trained, usually subconsciously, to communicate as literally and explicitly as possible. Good communication is all about getting your message across clearly and succinctly and accountability for accurate transmission rests with the speaker. We are often told 'if someone did not understand what you meant to say, it's because you did not communicate clearly'.

As a result, people from these societies tend to speak directly without mincing words. We prize the 'nothing to read between the lines' approach for its clarity, but not everyone sees it that way. People from the Middle East, for example, find Anglo-Saxon communication grating, specifically because it is so direct. I once had a Moroccan friend who felt this way, even after many years of living in Canada. He told me on more than one occasion,

"You Anglo-Saxons are so blunt!"

He did not mean it as a compliment. At the time, I found it hard to see his point, because to me, the way I communicated felt to the point, but not necessarily blunt and definitely not rude.

This difference of perspective stems from the fact that Morocco is a 'high-context' communication culture, where interpersonal relationships are extremely important and the harmony and well-being of the group is preferred over individual achievement[15], whereas Australia is 'low-context'. In low-context cultures, communication is more explicit and direct because individuals are not expected to have knowledge of each other's histories or background, and communication is not necessarily shaped by long-standing relationships between speakers. In high-context Middle Eastern and Asian cultures, messages are often conveyed implicitly, requiring the listener to read between the lines. Good communication is subtle, layered and often relies on lots of sub-text. Responsibility for transmission of a message is shared between the sender and the receiver.

For example, Arabs tend to talk around the point and expect the listener to be intuitive enough to discover the hidden message being communicated. They are more likely to use abstract ideas than concrete facts, particularly when bad news must be delivered. If a Lebanese or Saudi needs to refuse a request, he or she will rarely say 'no', as being so direct makes them feel extremely uncomfortable. Instead, he or she will drop hints and use indirect language to let you know that what you are asking cannot be done.

Saying 'no' between the lines is also common throughout Asia, especially when speaking to a boss or a client. If you work with a supplier or team member from China, Japan, the Philippines or Korea, you will find that people have a variety of ways to say, 'no'.

A question like, *"Can you complete this project by next week?"* may elicit a non-committal answer like *"I'll try my best"*, or *"We'll need to think about it"*, or a polite laugh that means *"It's never going to happen"*, or even a silence.

To a Westerner, this can feel like poor communication at best and evasiveness at worst. I have heard Western businesspeople, negotiating deals in the Middle East, ask,

"Why can't they just say what they mean?"

People from high-context cultures are also fond of talking about non-business topics in a business context. For example, the Finance Manager at Dearin & Associates is Indian and we meet every few weeks to review the finances. Even though our meeting is specifically finance-focused and time limited, he always makes a point of talking about other things that are happening in his life – the rate of COVID infections in India, what is happening with his family or property investments, the charitable project he set up. One time he even took our team on a virtual tour of a local temple. These themes often take up 30% of the meeting. As an Australian who is used to sticking with the meeting agenda, this can feel like a diversion, but I have come to appreciate the fact that this is how my colleague is building a relationship with my team, from thousands of kilometres away.

And it works.

These same patterns exist in other Asian cultures and as you can imagine, differences in communication styles can lead to serious misunderstanding when Westerners get talking to people from high-context societies. Being aware of the differences in the way in which high- and low-context cultures communicate will go quite a way towards helping you read a particular social or business context and to keeping you out of trouble, even before the commercial conversation begins.

If you come from a low-context culture, one of the ways you can improve communication with clients, suppliers and partners from high-context cultures is to practise 'listening between the lines' rather than taking everything at face value. Try to hear what is being implied, rather than focusing on the words themselves, and ask clarifying questions to tease out meaning.

On the other hand, if you come from a high-context culture, try to be as clear and transparent with your interlocutors as possible. State your objectives and opinions simply and clearly and show your cards upfront. At the end of a meeting or call, recap all the key points and agreed action steps and repeat these in your follow-up email. If you are ever unsure about what has been agreed or what you are expected to do, do not read between the lines, let people know that you are unsure and clarify their expectations.

A WORD ON EMAIL

The use of email is an area which can cause real problems in international business, because people have different expectations about how it is used. I want to highlight two issues: function and tone.

Westerners love email because it is fast, direct and it creates a written record of what happened, which we can use to hold others accountable – it complements our rules-based thinking. We feel comfortable dashing off short, snappy messages to colleagues as a way of managing work and driving projects forward.

Function

To people in relationship-based, high-context cultures, using email this way feels very perfunctory. In Middle Eastern cultures, for instance, people generally prefer to meet face-to-face (or on video or phone where an in-person meeting is not possible) to discuss work, because it is personal and helps to build a relationship – a key goal for them. Follow-up email is used sparingly, if at all. When I worked in Iraq, colleagues in various government ministries often did not reply to my emails, although they were amiable and easy enough to work with in-person.

In countries like Indonesia, the Western mania for writing everything down can feel like distrust. That is because where people agree a course of action in a meeting, they believe that the verbal commitment is sufficient and that black on white is only required where a person does not trust that someone will do what they have agreed to.

Tone

Without context, emails and text messages can be easily misinterpreted and problems can occur, even between cultures that are quite similar. I once heard an anecdote about two female colleagues, one British and the other Australian, who had come to dislike each other, at least partly thanks to their email communications.

The British woman would always begin her emails with a description of the weather in the UK and enquiries about her colleague's health, and the Australian would invariably reply with one sentence answers, completely bypassing all the peripheral detail. What probably felt to her like efficiency and clarity came across as rudeness and coldness to her slightly more high-context colleague on the other side of the world.

I recommend to my clients that they manage potential email problems by making email a secondary means of communication in their international business. My strong preference is that people communicate as much as they can via video (or phone at worst) and rely on email only to follow up and record outcomes, agreements and action points.

APPROACHES TO TIME

Time is another area where cultures tend to differ markedly in their approach. The American sociologist Edward T. Hall – who developed the theory of high- and low-context culture – concluded that two different orientations to time exist across the world: monochronic and polychronic. Monochronic approaches to time are linear, sequential and involve focusing on one thing at a time, whereas polychronic orientations to time involve simultaneous occurrences of many things and the involvement of many people. In a polychronic setting, the time it takes to complete an interaction is elastic and more important than any schedule. The Trompenaars' *Model of National Culture Differences* also divides approaches to time into sequential and synchronous, which map roughly to Hall's categories.

Western cultures tend to be monochronic/sequential whereas Middle Eastern and Latin American cultures are firmly polychronic/synchronous and Asian cultures are split between the two camps.

In monochronic or sequential cultures like Germany, Britain, Switzerland and the United States, people prefer to 'stick to the plan', to meet on time and for events to happen in the 'correct' order. They place a high value on planning, punctuality and staying on schedule because 'time is money'. Timetables must be adhered to.

By contrast, in polychronic or synchronous time cultures, meetings can start later and plans can be interrupted. People see the past, present, and future as interwoven periods. They often work on several projects at once, and view plans and commitments as flexible. I cannot tell you how many times I waited for meetings to start when I worked in Iraq, often with colleagues from the United States. While I was accustomed to laid-back Middle Eastern scheduling and prepared to cool my heels for a while, my American colleagues – who had not worked in the region before – found the delays maddening. This sometimes created a tense atmosphere in meetings, which is not a great way to begin.

As I mentioned above, there are a variety of approaches to time in Asia. Singaporeans value time and do not like to waste it. The Japanese are more concerned, not with how long something takes, but with how time is divided up in the interests of properness, courtesy and tradition.

The Chinese, like most Asians, 'walk around the pool' to make well-considered decisions, but they also have a keen sense of the value of time. This is apparent in their attitude towards taking up other people's time, for which they frequently apologise. For example, at the end of a meeting in China, it is customary to thank the participants for contributing their valuable time.

Punctuality is also important in China – more so than in many other Asian countries. Indeed, when meetings are scheduled between two people, it is not unusual for a Chinese to arrive 15 to 30 minutes early 'in order to finish the business before the time appointed for its discussion', so as not to steal any of the other person's time! It is also considered polite to announce, 10 or 15 minutes after a meeting has begun, that one will soon have to be going, so as to highlight a desire not to take too much of the other person's time. The Chinese person will not go until the transaction has been completed, but the point has been made.

There is something of a double standard at work here: the Chinese penchant for humility demands that the other person's time be seen as precious, but the Chinese also expect a liberal amount of time to be set aside for repeated consideration of the details of a transaction and to the careful nurturing of personal relationships surrounding the deal. Chinese people frequently complain that Americans doing business in China often have to catch their plane home 'in the middle of the discussion'. Whereas the Americans believe that the facts have been adequately discussed, the Chinese feel that they have not yet attained that degree of closeness that is (for them) the bedrock of the deal and of other transactions in the future.

Because approaches to time can be such a source of friction across cultures, it is worth the effort to contemplate your own approach to time and that of your counterpart as you do business overseas.

CHAPTER 9

MAKING THE MOST OF YOUR MARKET

CHAPTER 9

MAKING THE MOST OF YOUR MARKET – GETTING YOUR MODE OF MARKET ENTRY RIGHT

Once you have chosen a market to enter, you will need to decide on a mode of market entry. This essentially means working out how you will get your goods or services to the end user. Sounds simple, does it not? Do not be fooled!

Choosing a mode of market entry is an important decision. It is a key part of your international business model and will have a significant impact on costs to you and your client. Your mode of market entry will also affect the speed at which you can transact business and the amount of effort you will need to put in.

To move forward with an international expansion strategy, you need to be clear on how you will get to market and the steps in that process. Without clarity on the what and the how of the route to market, you may find yourself wasting a lot of time on tasks that do not contribute much to the success of the project. Especially at the early stages, your focus must be on building credibility and generating sales in the new geography.

Moreover, all modes of market entry involve resource commitments of some kind. If you make an initial choice that turns out to be wrong and have to design and implement a new route to market, you risk investing a lot of time and money for not much return.

Below are some of the big mistakes I see people making around choosing a mode market of entry.

- **They 'go with their gut'.** They take the most obvious path rather than canvassing a variety of options around entering the market.
- **They jump in 'boots and all'.** Rather than doing a series of small, modest experiments, they make a big upfront investment in one particular market entry strategy, before they have evidence that it will work for their situation.
- **They overlook the global logistics.** They forget to ask the simple questions about how their products will get there, or how they will deliver their service.

Making any one of these mistakes increases the odds that your launch into a new country will produce poor results. Making all three simultaneously could tank the venture.

What happens when you get your mode of market entry wrong?

Vanessa Garrard is an Australian entrepreneur who founded her group of companies in 2006. Today her focus is developing unique, design-led products for the consumer electronics and camping segments. One in two Australians owns a product that one of Vanessa's companies has produced. The Garrard Group has a global footprint, with key markets in the US and China, and sells to household names including Walmart, Best Buy, Argos, Kmart, Aldi and Target.

The Garrard Group entered the US market as an established business, with significant experience doing business internationally. Nonetheless, it was not all plain sailing. Vanessa says:

"My biggest lesson [about international market entry] was going to the US market. We'd have buyers from, for example Walmart – our big customers and the ones we wanted – talking to us directly and saying, 'Yes we want your product'.

"The challenge was that the [US] business model was so different that we underestimated how complex it was. We needed to have distributors on the ground, and local representatives, who the distributors deal with.

"In every other market, I could walk in with my sales team and we could deal directly with the buyers. You can't do that in the US. We thought we could, and so we spent all this money and set up our own team in the US and said, 'Let's just take our samples to those buyers and start doing meetings.'

"It turned out that the buyers wanted to know, 'Who's your rep? And who's your distributor? And what's the vendor code?'

"We didn't have all that and so we burnt a couple of hundred thousand dollars before we realised that our market entry strategy wasn't going to work.

"We pulled back, got our business model together again and went back in about a year-and-a-half later. At that point we found the right distributors on the ground, we found a good rep base and the orders started to come straight away then. Same product, same price point, same pitch – everything else was the same, we just didn't have the market entry strategy right."[16]

Market entry – 'What are my options?'

Modes of market entry range from low-risk to high-risk and include everything from simply selling internationally from your domestic website, acquiring a business overseas, or setting up an international company from scratch.

Broadly speaking, you can group these strategies into three categories: trading strategies, transfer strategies and investment strategies.

TRADING STRATEGIES

Trading strategies include direct exports (selling straight to the customer in the target market), e-commerce (selling online) and indirect exports (using an agent or a distributor).

These approaches are fairly low-risk and often do not require a large investment in setting up legal entities and offices in the country you are targeting. Trading strategies can be a good first step into a new market, because they allow you to test how well your products and services are received in that country. If all goes to plan, you might think about ramping up your operations, investing in a presence in-country, or even setting up a subsidiary company or manufacturing operation there.

E-commerce

Unless you live under a rock, you will know that e-commerce is using the internet to conduct business and sell goods or services. Almost any product or service can be offered via e-commerce, from books and music to financial services and plane tickets. Selling online is one of the most rapidly evolving and explosive trends in the commercial sphere and is revolutionising business, especially for small firms, both domestically and on an international scale.

Within the general category of e-commerce, there are several ways to sell goods or services internationally.

Sell from your own website into the target market

> Selling internationally from your existing company website hosted in your home market and created primarily for your domestic customers may be the easiest way of selling online, but it's often the least effective way too. Unless you have invested in a quality, international Search Engine Optimisation (SEO) strategy, your domestic website will not have much reach in another market. Its content and design might not appeal to customers there either. This can be especially true if you are selling in English, into a country which does not have English as its first language. Research demonstrates that people are around 71%

more likely to buy from a website that is in their mother tongue. Let's say you plan to target Chinese consumers. At a minimum, you should develop a Chinese language version of the website.

You should also remember that you want to make the online shopping experience as easy as possible for your customers. If you were going to sell to China, you should also consider enabling your site to accept Chinese credit card payments using a Chinese third-party payment platform such as Alipay or Tenpay.

Another downside of selling from your website at home is that the consumer will have to endure longer shipping times, transportation and import costs if the products are manufactured in your home country.

Finally, in some countries the government blocks or licenses overseas online selling websites. For example, China requires you to have a local ICP (Internet Content Provider) licence to sell there.

If you are going to use your own website to sell internationally, my strong recommendation is that you invest in SEO to maximise your site's visibility and search engine rankings.

Create a local website in the target market

A step up from selling from your domestic website is building a stand-alone website in your target market. If you go about it the right way, it can solve some of the customer accessibility, language barrier, overseas delivery fee and import tax problems I have just mentioned. However, it does not overcome the problem of limited reach. In some countries, your company must be a legal registered entity in-market to receive the necessary licences to build and maintain a website in that country. China, with its ICP licences, is one such market.

If you are going to set up a stand-alone website in your target market, you will need a team member who speaks the local language or an agency or consultant in-country to set up the site and localise and translate the content for you.

Sell your product through major e-commerce sites

If you prefer not to, there's no need to build and operate a stand-alone website to sell your goods into a new market. Major e-commerce sites (also known as online hypermarkets) like Amazon and Tmall are vertically integrated, multi-category marketplaces that purchase directly from suppliers for sale through their own network, much like a traditional 'bricks and mortar' retailer. In China, for example, around 90% of online transactions take place on open, third-party e-commerce sites.[17]

These sites can display products, receive orders and handle payments on behalf of merchants located in the target market and overseas. Selling wholesale to a hypermarket is done through negotiation with a procurement manager. The hypermarket manages the distribution and the shopfront, but you might need to provide marketing materials to promote your goods.

Hypermarkets and specialty sites (like Shopify and Etsy) also allow independent merchants to list products or operate shopfronts within their marketplaces.

Traditional direct exporting

For smaller operators, online sales can be a cost-effective means to establish a sales footprint in your target market, especially for niche products. If you are looking for higher turnover, you will probably need to investigate traditional direct exporting channels. Traditional direct exporting is shipping goods, providing services across borders or transferring technology from one country to another, directly to the end customer.

Where you are selling IP online, there is really no difference between 'selling online' as a mode and 'direct export'. They are the same thing.

Practically speaking, direct export is usually suitable for smaller quantities of unique products where a developed distribution network is not necessary, or for export of services or technology. The higher gains come from cutting out any intermediaries or agents etc., and avoiding the costs of setting up in the foreign market.

However, the downside is that companies that export directly are responsible for doing their own market research and carrying out all the necessary administrative requirements, such as:

- Ensuring that goods, service or technology can enter the market
- Meeting standards and certification requirements
- Meeting necessary labelling and licensing requirements.

They must also handle relations with freight forwarders and banks, and all customs procedures. We will cover these topics in greater detail in Chapter 10.

Indirect exporting

Another method to enter a foreign market is through an intermediary (an agent or a distributor) in that market. An agent works more closely with you whereas a distributor works more closely with your customers. Depending on the market, using a well-known agent or distributor can be one of the easier ways to enter the market for small and medium-sized firms.

Agents

An agent is your company's direct representative and is normally paid a monthly management fee and/or a commission to help represent and sell your product.

Agents act as the supplier's representative – they do not take ownership of the goods or services – and are generally paid by the exporter based on a commission of sales value generated. The exporter receives orders from the agent but then delivers goods or services directly to customers, invoices the customers, and collects payments from them. The exporter is also responsible for setting the selling price, although the agent will likely provide input on local market conditions to help the exporter decide on pricing.

Agents are generally based in the target market and often represent several complementary product or service lines. They may operate on an exclusive basis, as the sole agent for a company's goods or services in a specific export market, or as one of a number of agents for the exporter in that market – that is, on a non-exclusive basis.

Agents – pros and cons

Local agents have the knowledge and contacts to promote foreign products and help overcome barriers such as language and culture. They can also assist in keeping track of policy and regulatory updates, (both locally and nationally), collect market data and quickly respond to change. They are effectively your eyes and ears on the ground.

However, finding a dedicated, reliable, professional and credit-worthy agent or distributor takes work. Embassies and chambers of commerce are often contacted by agents who offer services, so it can be worth checking with your country's trade representation office in the target market to see if there is any specialised agent who has been introduced to them. Likewise, many agents and distributors will advertise their services online and can be met at relevant trade shows.

What makes a good agent?

- Knowledge of your product/service and its market
- Good references and previous experience (you should check to make sure)
- Language skills in a non-English speaking market (as well as English, if that is the language you work in)
- Strong networks and geographical coverage
- Support team, staff, sub-agents
- Soft skills and sales experience
- Ability to work with incentives (i.e., commission-based and subject to customer's payment first)
- Strong work ethic, such as the ability to prepare and submit reports and marketing plans, conduct training, work with limited marketing budgets and translate marketing materials
- Respect for the professional image of the company and transparency about any potential conflict of interest.

Companies should also be clear whether their agent represents any other companies and should consider starting with smaller tasks to see how he/she performs at the beginning.

Distributors

Using a distributor can also be a cost-effective and relatively easier way to enter a market.

A distributor buys your products and then sells them on to customers through a third party or directly. In some cases, the distributor may sell to other wholesalers who then sell to local retailers or end users. Their income comes from the difference between their buying and selling price.

Distributors may carry complementary and competing lines and usually offer after-sales service. Distributors are paid fees by adding a margin to products, and their fees are higher than those of agents because they usually carry inventory, extend credit for customers, and are responsible for marketing.

Because a distributor has more responsibilities in selling your product in-market than an agent, they require a higher margin. This may affect how you price your product. You will often need to absorb the distributor margin rather than adding it to the cost of your product, in order to keep pricing to the end customer competitive. Some exporters find that they are unable to use a distributor as their profit margin is too small to provide enough margin for the distributor and a competitive price for customers.

If you can find a reliable distributor and the numbers work, this approach can supercharge your reach in a new market. As a business owner or single salesperson, you can probably do a maximum of several hundred meetings a year to promote your product in an overseas market; whereas a distributor with dozens of representatives can do thousands or tens of thousands. If you get it right with a distributor, the potential for sales is exponentially greater than working alone, although margins are lower.

Exclusivity versus non-exclusivity

> Appointing an agent or distributor on an exclusive basis – where they have sole rights to sell your product within a defined territory – allows the agent or distributor to build their business free of competition in that territory.
>
> Many agents and distributors want exclusivity as they will invest effort and financial resources into building brand awareness to create a

market for your product. The stronger the brand reputation, the more valuable an exclusive arrangement will be.

It is a good idea to think through the issue of exclusivity versus non-exclusivity carefully before entering into negotiations with potential partners. Be careful about signing exclusive agreements which put the future of your business in that market completely in your partner's hands. This puts your business at significant risk if the relationship goes sour, particularly because, in some countries, distribution agreements are very difficult to terminate.

If you intend to agree to an exclusive arrangement, you should establish performance measures, and include a termination clause for non-performance in the distribution agreement.

TIP If a distributor insists on exclusivity, agree to it only for a limited period (six months) and make continuing exclusivity subject to the achievement of milestones.

CASE STUDY: Ego Pharmaceuticals

Alan Oppenheim, Managing Director of Ego Pharmaceuticals, describes the company's experience of using distributors as 'highly variable.' He says,

"We still have distributors in some nations – great distributors, who have been strong partners, who understand us and we understand them, and together we work the relationship strongly. But in many countries, we have outgrown distributors.

"Distributors vary hugely. The benefit of using a distributor, particularly in the beginning, is that they are easy. They look after the sales and marketing for your brand and that is an easy start to doing the export ... but one of the big challenges of using a distributor is that a distributor always has lots of principals that they are working for. So you need to ask yourself, how are you going to inspire that distributor

to spend more sales and marketing time on your brand, rather than the other brands?

"And, can you? Has the distributor got sufficient resources to do all the brands? And that is a question you need to keep asking, because distributors tend to add more and more principals without necessarily increasing their staff. So, your whole brand can gradually get diluted."

When it comes to managing the distributor relationship, Oppenheim says:

"It takes a lot of time. I think managing a distributor takes more time than managing your own staff. Remember that when you have a distributor, you are delegating the responsibility for your brand to that distributor, which is a huge responsibility. We have discovered that when we have replaced distributors with our own people, that a particular distributor may have treated our brand vastly differently to how we treated it. And that is a challenge, because then, when you go in with your own people, you have to unlearn the market, before you then educate the market about who Ego really is.

"Trying to nurture and inspire that distributor is about spending time with them, sometimes it might be incentives for the sales team, sometimes it's about asking the question, 'How can I inspire you?'

"Sometimes it's setting KPIs in your agreement with the distributor – that the distributor will commit a certain number of staff full-time for your brands – if that can work, it depends how big you are. When you are starting from scratch, that can be a whole lot harder. It varies. In the end, we have found having our own people, in most countries, means that we lift the growth from, in some cases 2% or 5% to about 20%.

"Distributors are really useful in the beginning, but I recommend that companies – as they grow – should have a long-term plan to grow beyond a distributor, unless the distributor is great."

CHOOSING AN AGENT OR DISTRIBUTOR

When it comes to choosing a distributor, Alan Oppenheim describes it as:

> *"More complicated and more messy than recruiting for staff ... if we are going into a brand new country that we do not know, we'll talk to Austrade (Australia's Federal trade promotion agency) and we'll talk to the Victorian government ... and they will give you information about the country – in our case,*
>
> ***'Where do you buy your skin products?'***
>
> ***'Do you go to a pharmacy?'***
>
> ***'How do patients get their pharmaceutical products?'***
>
> *"We'll also go into the marketplace and talk in the shops and try to understand. We'll talk to people about prospective distributors to try and get lists of them. In some cases, we have used a consultant.*
>
> *"One of the things I have found is, if a distributor is similar in size and culture to Ego, then the relationship is better. They would understand our problems better, our strengths and our challenges and the empathy was just a bit stronger. I have worked with very small distributors, I have worked with a distributor listed on the local stock exchange. The latter is not one that I would recommend particularly, because there were then issues with communication. So, it's trying to find a distributor that you feel comfortable with ... that has the skills and has the values. And you have to make sure they have to invest in your brand and to pay the bills ... there's a whole suite of things you have to consider in selecting a distributor.*
>
> *"The most important factor in choosing an agent or distributor is that you can establish a close working relationship. Business is much easier to transact if you enjoy working with each other and so you have to be able to build high levels of trust and communicate regularly."*

Before choosing an overseas partner you should undertake a rigorous research process and speak with a range of potential agents or distributors – perhaps four or five – before narrowing the list. Before making a final decision ask your potential partner for trade references, and also consider using a professional credit checking agency to confirm the potential partner's financial stability.

Wherever possible, you should meet potential partners in their own market rather than in your home country. They should show you the market first-hand, which will give you a feel for how well they know the market and give you a chance to get to know them better as a person.

Exporters who rely only on email communication with overseas partners often have misunderstandings leading to problematic relationships. While email is ideal for confirming discussions, meeting in person or via video in the early stages can go a long way towards reducing misunderstandings.

Remember that you are relying on your representative's local knowledge and contacts to win business in the market, so make sure that the relationship is real. You may need to meet several times to build a relationship and work through the fundamentals of how you will work together and what should be included in an agreement.

Before drafting an agreement, you should be in agreement about who does what. Then you should engage legal advice in order to have a contract drawn up. Drafting agreements and making changes when two parties have differing views on core issues can be a waste of time and money, so it is wiser to agree on the big issues first, then start the legal work.

TRANSFER STRATEGIES

As companies grow and develop a reputation for quality products and services, their intellectual property becomes more valuable. Transfer strategies like licensing and franchising – which were once the exclusive domain of multinationals – have been adopted as a means of expansion by niche-market businesses.

Franchising

Franchising[18] is a legal and business model designed to achieve multi-unit expansion. In an international context, it can be a strategic way to reduce dependence on domestic demand and grow new, future revenue and profit centres worldwide.

Franchising typically involves a franchisor who grants to an individual or company (the franchisee) the right to run a business selling a product or service under the franchisor's successful business model and identified by the franchisor's trademark or brand.

The franchisor charges an initial upfront fee to the franchisee, payable upon the signing of the franchise agreement. Other fees such as marketing, advertising or royalties may be applicable, largely based on how the contract is negotiated and set up.

Advertising, training and other support services are made available by the franchisor.

Compared to organic expansion where you invest in and open multiple locations yourself, franchising allows you to recruit others – your future franchisees – to invest their capital, time and managerial effort in establishing new locations using your trademarks, systems and brand.

Franchising – pros and cons

Franchising enables you to grow internationally, by replicating multiple units of your business across new locations. Franchisees provide the capital required to expand to multiple geographies by buying a franchise.

Because franchising is all about unit expansion, replicating business systems, sources of supply, and uniformity of operations, it allows you to increase your purchasing power and achieve economies of scale with suppliers and vendors. These economies of scale can even extend to marketing where you and franchisees will be pooling resources and establishing common funds.

Franchising also creates a supply of skilled, trained, motivated managerial talent, which is key to scaling a company across multiple international markets. Franchisees supply the managerial talent needed for new locations and, because they buy into the business, they have a vested interest in its success.

In addition to entering new overseas markets with additional customers, international franchising can also offer what is called foreign master franchise owners. These individuals are typically local to the country and understand the political and bureaucratic subtleties of the market far better than any outsider.

Foreign master franchise owners pay a hefty upfront fee to acquire a designated geographic area or, in some instances, an entire country where they operate as a mini or sub-franchise company, selling franchises, collecting royalties, training the owners and overseeing all other related matters. They can even open units by themselves. In general, a specified number of franchises must be outlined for the exclusive right to use the business model in an entire country.

Despite the advantages, franchising is not all upside

One of the key drawbacks is loss of control. Compared to organic expansion where you own every location, when you franchise you are giving up some control to your franchisees who will own and operate their franchised locations. While franchisees will be required to complete your training and meet your standards and specifications, ultimately, they will need to have a significant impact on your business operations in multiple countries.

Franchise sales are competitive too. Once you franchise your business the next step is to sell franchises to qualified franchisees that have capital. While you may have organic interest from individuals that know your business and want to buy a franchise, long-term, you will need to attract qualified franchisees and this means that you will need to invest in marketing, public relations, and relationships with franchise brokers.

Franchising requires ongoing investment. Even after you make the initial investment in franchising your business, franchising will require you to invest time and capital on an ongoing basis, to build up your franchise system. The success of your first number of franchisees will determine the growth and trajectory of your new franchise network.

You cannot just go it alone. Because franchising is a regulated industry, you will need to work with a franchise lawyer to develop a franchise offering, comprised of a franchise disclosure document (FDD), before you can offer or sell a franchise. You will also need to ensure that you comply with franchise laws in your country.

Licensing

Licensing is where the exclusive owner of intellectual property rights (IPR) such as technology or patents, trademarks or copyrights gives another entity permission to use the IPR on agreed terms and conditions including the payment of royalties. Licensing can cover several areas including:

- **Technology transfer** – including patents, designs, software, and know-how
- **Copyrights** – original works of authorship fixed in any tangible form
- **Trademarks** – words, names or symbols identifying goods made or sold, distinguishing them from others.

Small companies often lack the financial, physical or human resources to commercialise their IP and licensing can be a means of solving that problem. For example, a small company that has developed a new method for making petrol from crude oil is likely to license it to an established company, because building a refinery just is not feasible for a small business.

Licensing is also a way to establish a foothold in multiple countries. In the US, in particular, it is common for companies to license their technology to unrelated foreign companies that use the technology to manufacture and sell products in a country or group of countries defined in the licensing agreement.

How does licensing work?

Technology licensing is a contractual arrangement in which the licensor's patents, trademarks, service marks, copyrights, trade secrets, or other intellectual property are sold or made available to a licensee.

The parties negotiate the compensation in advance. Payment may take the form of a lump-sum royalty, a running royalty (based on volume of production), or a combination of both.

Licensing – pros and cons

A technology licensing agreement can be an attractive option for a small company because it usually enables the business to enter a foreign market quickly. It also poses fewer financial and legal risks than owning and operating a foreign manufacturing facility or participating in an overseas joint venture. Licensing may also enable a company to overcome many tariff and non-tariff barriers that can hamper the export of foreign-manufactured products.

However, technology licensing also has some drawbacks as a mode of market entry. The owner's control over the technology is weakened because it has been transferred to another company and licensing usually produces smaller profits for the owner company than exporting actual goods or services. Importantly, in some countries, adequately protecting the licensed technology from unauthorised use by third parties may be difficult.

The last word on transfer strategies

Transfer strategies can provide an easy route to market, because the licensee or franchisee does a lot of the leg work and there is no need for you, as the foreign owner of the product, to build a distribution network in-market. This means that the initial cost in terms of time, resources and financial outlay to set up is low. Another plus is that local franchisees and licensees have local knowledge which can help in reaching new markets and finding new partners, which may also speed up your entry to the market.

However, there are some potential downsides. Licensing and franchising means allowing a third party to use your intellectual property rights for profit. This means that you automatically have less control over the business model than you would if you were selling your IP yourself.

Because you are handing over your IP to a third party, there is a risk that it could be copied or stolen (especially in countries where IP rights are not vigorously protected) or that your reputation could be spoiled by dubious partners.

And, although transfer strategies are low-cost, they typically provide lower returns than setting up a presence in the target market, so the initial savings you make may not be enough to offset lower long-term profits.

INVESTMENT STRATEGIES

Investment strategies include strategic alliances, joint ventures, mergers and acquisitions and establishing a presence in-market. This category covers a range of options and levels of risk. At one end of the scale you have strategic alliances, which can be as simple as a temporary collaboration between two companies. At the other, there are mergers (two companies joining forces permanently), acquisitions (one company buying out another), or setting up a subsidiary or a branch of your domestic company in the new country.

There are a range of reasons for a company to consider making direct investments in a foreign market.

- Some governments prohibit or limit imports of goods produced in other countries, but a company can build a production site in the foreign market and produce locally.
- Producing goods in the target market avoids import duties and other taxes and the requirement for import permits.
- Companies can obtain the services of skilled employees in the target market or gain intelligence held by people in that market.
- In certain countries, companies can take advantage of lower costs, such as cheaper labour, and in doing so become more competitive.

Strategic alliances

A strategic alliance is a relationship between two or more organisations that – through the combination of resources – can create significant and sustainable value for everyone involved. That is a very broad definition, but we can narrow it down somewhat by applying five key criteria developed by Cisco, a leader in the strategic alliance space. According to

Cisco, to be a strategic alliance, an arrangement must deliver:

- **Significant business impact with sustainable value** – *significant* is always defined relative to the stakeholders and *sustainable* means generating acceptable profit margins over a multi-year period
- **Broad and deep initiatives** – *broad* means several and *deep* means significant initiatives in the alliance that cut across the value chains of both companies
- **Strong organisational commitment** – from the CEO down
- **Substantial investment by both companies** – investment can be capital, people, IP, or all three
- **Strategic alignment and fit** – the companies' strategies in the target space must be well aligned. Although the cultures may be different, the companies must be able to establish an environment of trust.

Strategic alliances – pros and cons

Like any international expansion model, there are pros and cons. On the upside, an in-country alliance partner will already have networks and market intelligence that it would otherwise take you years to recreate. A strategic alliance enables cost sharing and allows each party to capitalise on the strengths of the other.

On the downside, a strategic alliance always entails the risk of conflict between partners – not to mention the creation of a future local, or international, competitor if the alliance does not last.

Some years ago, I had a bad experience with a strategic alliance in the Middle East. I was approached by the founder of a firm that provided services that were complementary to the work my team did. He asked whether we would consider partnering with his company to introduce companies to investors in the Middle East. I did not know the guy from a bar of soap, but as he was based in the Middle East and I was in Australia, the idea seemed to make sense.

Stupidly, I did not do much due diligence on the guy or his firm, and started working with him several months later.

As time passed, I began to realise that we did not share the same values – I was committed to providing great service and results for clients, my partner was more interested in collecting fees. I was not impressed with his work and he saw my company as a competitor to his. Trust eventually broke down between us and we went our separate ways – it was a sobering experience and a lesson in how not to do strategic alliances.

What does a great strategic alliance look like?

Here are some examples of international strategic alliances that have paid off in a big way.

- **Spotify and Uber.** US rideshare giant Uber's alliance with Swedish music streaming platform Spotify is one for the history books. The partnership lets Uber riders easily stream their Spotify music library whenever they take a ride. This helps the Uber experience feel more personalised, and encourages Uber customers to subscribe to Spotify Premium.

  Uber's competitors do not have a similar personalised music experience, so the alliance gives Uber an advantage over similar services. And since not all Uber riders have Spotify, and not all Spotify users ride with Uber, both brands gain access to new, broader audiences.

- **BMW and Louis Vuitton.** Although they might seem very different, French fashion house Louis Vuitton and German carmaker BMW are both exclusive luxury brands that focus on craftsmanship.

  Because of their shared audience, goals and values, the two brands partnered up to create a collection of Louis Vuitton bags, custom made to pair with the BMW i8 sports car. According to Patrick-Louis Vuitton, Head of Special Orders at Louis Vuitton,

  > *"This collaboration with BMW epitomises our shared values and creativity, technological innovation and style."*

  The bags' sleek black outer colour and electric blue lining match the car's design perfectly, and they are made of an innovative, unlikely material – carbon fibre, just like the i8's passenger cell. Plus, the four-piece set of bags fits perfectly into the i8's parcel shelf. The set may have retailed for a whopping USD 20,000, but that is a reasonable price for someone who is already buying a car for more than USD 135,000.

A client of mine, Jeremy Streten, used a strategic alliance to launch his law tech product, the Business Legal Lifecycle platform, into two key markets, the United Kingdom and the United States. The product helps business owners diagnose what kind of legal support their company requires, before engaging a lawyer. Lawyers and accountants can direct clients to the platform as a precursor to paying for advice. Jeremy created alliances with professional services firms in Britain and the States, enabling him to reach many more end users than he would have been able to alone.

Joint ventures

A joint venture is when a separate company is created and jointly owned by two or more independent entities to achieve an objective.

International joint ventures (IJV) are used in a wide variety of manufacturing, mining and service industries, and they frequently involve technology licensing by the parent company to the joint venture. Cross-border joint ventures are especially popular in Asia, due to the restrictions on foreign ownership rights in some sectors of large emerging economies like China, India and Thailand.[19]

Joint ventures – pros and cons

International joint ventures enable faster, less expensive access to foreign markets than can be achieved by purchasing an existing company in the jurisdiction or starting a new venture.[20] They can help a business grow faster, increase productivity and generate greater profits. A successful joint venture can offer:

- A means to enter international markets while reducing risk
- Quick access to new markets and distribution networks via your local partner's established networks
- Access to the knowledge, know-how and contacts of a local

partner who can add value by filling gaps in your knowledge relating to the customs and tastes of local consumers

- Local partner proficiency in the local language and customs
- Sharing of risks and costs with a partner
- Access to greater resources, including specialised staff, technology and finance.

Additionally, joint ventures often enable growth without having to borrow funds or look for outside investors. You may be able to:

- Use your joint venture partner's customer database to market your product
- Offer your partner's services and products to your existing customers
- Join forces in purchasing, research and development.

A joint venture can also be very flexible. For example, the structure can have a limited life span and only cover part of what you do, limiting the commitment and exposure for both parties.

These benefits can be especially critical to a small or medium-sized business that does not have the capital, resources or expertise necessary to pursue the opportunity unless it can share the risks and costs through an alliance like an international joint venture. IJVs allow the partners to move quickly, cost effectively and with credibility (provided by the reputation of the resident partner) in the local marketplace. The parties to an IJV can also take advantage of complementary lines of business and synergies that may exist between them.

But... you must get it right!

On the other hand, partnering with another business can be complex and it takes time and effort to build the right business relationship. That is one of the reasons that joint ventures can be risky. Approximately 50% of all joint ventures fail and, in India for example, 90% of joint ventures between Indian and foreign companies fail.

Here are some of the key risks and drawbacks to the joint venture model:

- **Clashes in corporate culture and disputes about control** and operational decisions are common. For example, which financial, ethics, or operational policies should the new joint venture follow? If the parties disagree about strategies and investment, who should make the final decision?
- **Finding balance is often difficult.** Too little oversight can mean lack of direction, or damage to your company's brand or reputation. Too much oversight or control can result in frustration, and value destruction rather than creation.[21]
- **Joint ventures are often difficult to capitalise as an entity,** particularly in respect to debt, because they are finite in their duration and therefore lack permanence. Unless an IJV is adequately capitalised, its debt financing, if available at all, may have to be guaranteed, in whole or in part, by the joint venture partners, which can increase their level of risk in the venture.
- Depending on the country, you may be **limited to a minority share** in the joint venture.

Problems are likely to arise in a joint venture if:

- The objectives of the venture are not clear and communicated to everyone involved
- The partners have different objectives for the joint venture
- The partners bring in different levels of expertise, investment or assets
- Different cultures and management styles result in poor integration and cooperation
- The partners do not provide sufficient leadership and support in the early stages.

When does a joint venture make sense?

A cross-border joint venture could make sense for your company if you:

- Have identified a high-potential marketplace and a good prospect partner, or local regulations require you to have one

- Have substantial international expansion experience – joint ventures are usually a bad option for newbies
- Are able to partner effectively, while balancing risk against control
- Can afford to provide the necessary capital and internal and external resources
- Are seeking a lower-risk, albeit slower, way to make local acquisitions.

Making a joint venture work

In the initial phases, success in a joint venture depends to some extent on thorough research and analysis of aims and objectives. For the venture to work at all, you must effectively communicate the business plan to everyone involved.

Each of the businesses involved needs to understand what it wants from the relationship. Normally, you will be looking for a partner who is compatible with your business. This partner can be:

- **A larger business** – which can offer you their resources such as a strong distribution network in the target market, specialist employees and finance.
- **A smaller business** – which may be more flexible, innovative or simply provide you with access to new products or intellectual property.
- **A supplier** – which can offer you its knowledge of new technologies, the local market and a better quality of service, in return for a guaranteed volume of sales to you.

As well as your own needs, you should think about what your joint venture partner will be hoping to get from the arrangement. You will need to agree objectives that suit both of you, as well as things like:

- The structure of your joint venture
- Who will manage the venture and how
- Who will finance the venture and how
- The assets and resources you will both contribute
- Who will own any intellectual property that comes out of the venture

- How you will share profits and any potential losses
- How you will handle any potential disputes.

When a cross-border joint venture is created, there are also a range of complex employment, tax, financial and compliance issues to be considered – as well as preparing for possible termination or acquisition – that can be costly to set up. You should always retain experienced legal counsel to draft your joint venture agreement. It requires an investment, but can prevent a lot of headaches if things do not go according to plan.

Once the structure is up and running, there is still a likelihood of early problems. A significant portion of cross-border alliances suffer financial and operational challenges during the first years of operation. The key to their continued survival and success after 'hitting the wall' requires ownership flexibility and long-term support.

It is important to keep in mind from the start that joint ventures are generally temporary arrangements, and that they normally end either when the objectives of the venture are met, or things go awry. That is why you should plan your exit strategy from the beginning, to make sure you get a return on your investment in the joint venture.

Bear in mind that when a joint venture dissolves, the technology and know-how shared with your local partner can create a strong competitor, particularly in countries with weak intellectual property protection.

Mergers and acquisitions

If your company already has a track record of international sales, a merger or acquisition can be a good way to expand your international footprint. For example, one of my clients – the manufacturer of a welding product – is acquiring a company in the US that produces the fluid that the machine needs to operate. This will enable my client to significantly increase its sales of consumables across North America.

It is worth noting that, although mergers and acquisitions (M&A) are usually bundled into one term, they are fundamentally very different creatures.

In a merger, one company absorbs the other and it ceases to exist. In an acquisition, one company obtains a majority stake in another company, through a cash sale, shares or equity. However, the target business retains its name and legal structure.

Mergers and acquisitions – pros and cons

What are some of the reasons that you might consider an international merger or acquisition? And what are some of the drawbacks?

Economies of Scale

Underpinning all of M&A activity is the promise of economies of scale. The benefits that come from becoming bigger include:

- Increased access to capital
- Lower costs as a result of higher volume
- Better bargaining power with distributors[22]

Greater value

A merger or acquisition adds more value to the combined entity than either individual company can produce on its own.

New markets at lower cost

A merger or acquisition provides almost instant access to a new market for the party trying to enter that country. By joining forces with another entity which knows the target market, you save enormous amounts of time and money, which would otherwise be spent learning the market and 'reinventing the wheel' when it comes to doing business there.

Increased market share

One of the more common motives for M&A is increased market share. Historically, retail banks have looked at geographical footprint as being key to achieving market share. The Spanish retail bank, Santander, has made the acquisition of smaller banks an active policy. Consequently, it has become one of the world's largest retail banks.

Tax advantages

Some governments offer tax cuts when a merger or acquisition is completed. For example, Singapore is one jurisdiction that is extremely friendly to M&A. Opening a business in Singapore by merging or acquiring a smaller existing company can attract substantial tax advantages.[23]

Access to talent

M&A allow the acquiring company to immediately access an established workforce with the skills it needs in the new geography, rather than having to build its talent pool from the ground up.

Accelerated strategy implementation

M&A are sometimes the best way to achieve a long-term strategy in a much shorter timeframe. Suppose a British company wanted to enter the Canadian market; it could build from the ground up and hope that it reached the desirable scale in five to ten years. Or it could purchase a business, and leverage its established client base, distribution, and brand value.

Despite the benefits of M&A, there are a range of factors which make it a reasonably high-risk option for international expansion.

Time-consuming and complex

M&A have a reputation for being lengthy and complicated because the process usually involves multiple parties and a complex decision-making process.

Employee upheaval

M&A can create distress within the employee base of each organisation, as staff deal with the uncertainty and change that shifts in company ownership, structure and management bring.

More debt

Acquiring another business is a relatively expensive process and usually increases the amount of debt the acquiring company owes.

Clash of cultures

Merging two businesses frequently highlights and aggravates differences in the corporate culture of each company. These are often difficult to resolve and in extreme cases can lead to an eventual unwinding of the deal.

Offshore incorporation

Once your company has experience in international sales, the next step may be to set up a more permanent presence in a particular country or region. If you are planning to set up your own company in a new international market, the options vary from country to country.

In many markets, the possibilities range from a single-person sales office to full manufacturing operations. You do not always have to set up a fully separate legal entity to start with. It might be sufficient to set up a representative office, and graduate to another form of company later. When choosing which kind of legal entity to establish, keep in mind that your choice will dictate what functions the office is allowed to carry out, and how you are taxed.

Representative office

A representative office usually has limited authority to carry out some business development, but contracts can only be signed with the company's head office. On the other hand, its tax liability might be much less onerous than that of a legally registered branch.

Branch offices and subsidiaries

The definition of branch offices and subsidiaries varies depending on the country. Generally speaking, a branch office is not a separate legal entity of the parent corporation. Accordingly, operating a branch office is essentially having the foreign parent corporation operating in the target market, which can expose your core business to increased legal risk in the foreign jurisdiction.

A subsidiary, on the other hand, is a separate legal entity from the parent. Although it is owned by the parent corporation, it has a separate legal personality and provides the parent company with an extra layer of protection from risk in the international market.

In some countries, such as some of the Arab Gulf states, the law requires that locally-incorporated companies in some sectors are at least 51% owned by a local national or local company. In these jurisdictions, you will need a local partner or nominee structure, unless you set up in a free-trade zone.

Offshore incorporation – pros and cons

- **Complete control and autonomy.** Unlike the scenario in which you merge with another offshore entity, or acquire a smaller international company, offshore incorporation gives you complete control over day-to-day operations in overseas markets. If the business does not succeed, you have the ability to unilaterally wind up the company and withdraw from the market.
- **Asset protection**. An offshore company can also be used as a mode of asset protection. For example, you might choose to run international sales through an offshore structure to protect the parent company in case of legal action in another jurisdiction. Or, you may opt to house your intellectual property in a vehicle in another jurisdiction, to protect your business' inherent value in the event that your company is sued.
- **Tax minimisation**. To attract inbound investment, some countries promote attractive tax regimes on defined activities or sectors. In jurisdictions like Vanuatu, Samoa, the Bahamas, Cayman Islands, Ireland, UAE and Switzerland, commercial laws and policies are geared to minimise the taxes levied on local corporations. To benefit from reduced taxes, businesses use lawful foreign incorporations to vest their assets.[24]

Other low-tax or no-tax jurisdictions, like Anguilla, provide shielding and exemptions from stamp duties and excise on transactions. They also waive tax on net profits, capital gains tax on foreign investment, salaries and transmission of shares to new holders, all of which help to reduce the business operating expenditure.

Privacy and confidentiality

Another reason to incorporate offshore is that when you use an offshore corporate structure, it separates you from your business or assets and liabilities. Your offshore entity takes on a legal identity separate from those who own it.

Many offshore financial centres – including a number of the jurisdictions mentioned above – complement their investment-friendly policies with stringent corporate and banking data confidentiality. Company registries in these countries are not open to the public, and details relating to a company and its accounts are not publicly available unless there is a criminal investigation. These shielding mechanisms provide confidentiality for directors and shareholders. While each country has its own level of transparency, you are more able to remain anonymous (depending on the country and your tax obligations with the country where you live) with your assets and company structure at arm's length.

Simple Corporate Regulations

A number of jurisdictions, including New Zealand and Singapore, have created corporate laws that attract foreign companies and individuals by simplifying regulations and by lowering the amount of bureaucratic red tape. Others, like the Cook Islands, have no requirements for auditing nor financial reporting.

While there are many good reasons to consider incorporating internationally, there are also some downsides.

Resource intensive

Setting up and staffing a company in-country requires substantial resources, so the exposure to risk is higher than some other forms of international business.

Going it alone

When you incorporate internationally, you are essentially starting your business again – in a new country. Without a local partner to assist you with administration, connect you with clients and suppliers and advise on customs and culture, you may find yourself dealing with a lot of complexity and a vastly increased workload.

Higher costs and liability

Although offshore incorporation is less expensive and risky than a merger or acquisition, it is more expensive and riskier than acting through an agent or with a partner.

Proving ownership may be difficult

If you incorporate in a jurisdiction with stringent privacy and banking rules or no public registers, proving ownership of a company registered offshore can be difficult. While anonymity can be an advantage for overseas companies, it can become a disadvantage if the owner later wants to declare themselves as the beneficial owner.[25]

Bringing the money back exposes you to taxation

Depending on the jurisdiction and company structure that you choose, the remittance and distribution of the assets and income of an offshore company can have downsides. Once funds reach the country in which the shareholders are headquartered, they are subject to taxation and in some cases double taxation, which can negate the initial benefits of a low-tax or no-tax environment.

To sum up

With the exception of strategic alliances, investment strategies usually involve higher initial costs and risks, and are usually more appropriate for companies with significant international experience and a demonstrated track record in the target market. If you do choose to pursue an investment strategy, engaging advisors who can provide sound legal and tax advice is a must.

HOW DO I CHOOSE A MODE OF MARKET ENTRY?

As you can see, when it comes to market entry, you have a range of options at your disposal. Before you start drilling down into the process of selecting a way to get your products to the international market, it can be helpful to stand back and consider which types of mode of market entry are likely to work best for you. Take into account things like:

- The size of your business
- Your international experience to date
- Your appetite for risk
- The type of products you sell
- The conditions in the market you have chosen
- The time and resources available to you to manage the day-to-day running of your international business.

Let's look at a few of those considerations now.

The size of your company

Different modes of market entry require different levels of effort and bring different levels of return. Smaller companies are often less inclined to take big risks than larger firms, simply because they do not have the resources and cash reserves to pursue high-risk strategies.

If you are part of a small business, you will probably want to begin your international expansion with a series of small, cost-effective experiments, to test the hypothesis that your business has what it takes to be internationally successful. For example, rather than immediately setting up a subsidiary in your target market, you might trial exporting goods or services there until you are confident that there is a sizeable market for your products – at which point you can look at ramping up operations and putting a team on the ground.

Time and resources available within your firm

Related to the size of your company is how much time and resources your team can realistically spend on an international expansion at the outset of the project.

Make sure that you choose a mode of market entry that will allow you to test your international market without stretching your team so far that you end up damaging the domestic business as well as the international venture. Think about what kind of inputs are realistic given the size of your company and what level of risk you can accept. You will also need a clear understanding of what sort of return you need to make the risk worthwhile.

The nature of your products

The nature of your products will also influence how you go to market.

- Are they physical or intangible?
- Will they require customs clearance, or can they travel freely across the internet?
- Will they be sold from supermarket shelves or go straight to the client's inbox?
- Are they likely to require after-sales service and support?

To some extent, you might be able to replicate the model you use at home to market, sell and distribute products in your new market, but you need to account for the added complexity of operating in a new country. You will not necessarily know 'how things work', you will not have the same familiarity with customer preferences, you might not be across the local regulations in your sector, or be able to get up to speed easily, especially if there is a language barrier involved. And you will probably not have the same networks and ability to 'get things done' – at least not straight away. So, it could make sense to get support, either by partnering with a local company, using an agent or distributor, or hiring a sales or customer service team, in-country.

Business conditions and regulations

Restrictions on establishing foreign-owned entities in the country you are targeting, requirements for permits, licences or other non-tariff barriers that make it difficult for your company to operate there in its own right will all have an impact on how you can enter the market.

You might need to appoint a distributor or team up with a local partner, rather than going it alone. Alternatively, and depending on the country, you might look at setting up in a free-trade zone, where the regulations are less restrictive.

Control of your product and protecting your IP

If you are concerned that your IP might be stolen and/or copied in the market you are planning to work in, you may want to steer clear of a licensing strategy, which drastically reduces your control over the product and intellectual property. This is especially important if enforcing your IP rights will be a challenge in that country. In this case, a low-risk strategy like direct exporting could be the way to go in the first instance.

International experience

If this is your first foray into international business, you might be feeling a little less than 100% confident about the process of getting your goods or services into your target market. And you would be right – this is a complex area.

As you ponder your market entry options, ask yourself:

"Do I have an in-depth knowledge of the market I am planning to work in or sell to?"

"Do I understand its business culture, regulatory environment and banking system?"

"Do I know how best to reach my prospective clients?"

If the answer to these questions is 'No', you might want to team up with someone who knows your target market well, and this should influence your choice of market entry option.

Appetite for risk

Different modes of market entry involve different levels of effort and risk and produce different levels of return. You should choose a mode with an awareness of what level of risk you are prepared to accept and keep in mind what sort of return you need to make the exercise worthwhile.

Whatever you do, do not rush the decision about mode of market entry. If you get it wrong it could be costly to reverse.

CHAPTER 10

GETTING IT THERE – THE LOGISTICS LOW-DOWN

CHAPTER 10

GETTING IT THERE – THE LOGISTICS LOW-DOWN

Congratulations – you have made a sale to buyers overseas. Now, how do you get the goods to your new international customer efficiently, competitively, securely and legally?

It is time to talk about global logistics.

What do I need to know about moving goods?

When you are shipping a product overseas as part of a commercial transaction, it is important to understand the basic principles of both sea and air cargo. Your product may be suited only for ocean shipping or for airfreight, or both, and rates can vary when new capacity is offered on trade routes and when new markets are serviced.

There are also packing, labelling, documentation and insurance requirements that you will need to be aware of and comply with.

HOW CAN I SEND MY GOODS OVERSEAS?

There are three or four main options when it comes to sending goods overseas. You can use express delivery or mail services, an international freight forwarder, or arrange your own shipping. Depending on which country you are based in, you may also be able to access the services of Shippers' Associations.

Air or sea?

The choice between air and sea freight normally depends on your shipment's size, weight and contents, and on how fast your goods need to arrive.

Under normal conditions, shipping by air often makes a lot of sense for small shipments. It may cost more, but your goods will arrive within days rather than weeks. In sectors like retail, where quick turnover is key, or electronics, which benefit from air freight's heightened security, air is usually the right choice.

COVID-19 has dramatically increased the cost of air freight, for two reasons. Restrictions on passenger transport have reduced space available for shipping, and what is left is prioritised for medical supplies.

However, airlines are flying, and even augmenting cargo planes with passenger planes so, if you need to, you can still ship by air.

Air freight is the best option when:

- The cost of shipping is less than 15–20% of the value of the goods.
- You are shipping goods that are not considered hazardous materials.

Ocean freight on the other hand is typically much cheaper than air freight, especially for larger shipments. Ocean freight prices are also far less volatile than air freight prices. If you have time to wait for your goods to arrive, try to ship by ocean when possible.

Ocean freight is the best option when:

- You have a lot of goods to move and you are looking for more capacity and value – one container can hold 10,000 beer bottles!
- Time is not of the essence. Ocean freight is usually much slower than air, and customs issues and port holdups can cause additional delays. However, Express LCL (less-than-container-load) – increasingly available on more routes and by more forwarders – often guarantees a delivery date and is often not that much slower than air.

- Sustainability matters. Ocean freight has a much better carbon footprint than air freight.

How do I negotiate the best freight rate for my cargo?

The cost of freight has increased astronomically since 2020, when the COVID-19 pandemic caused major disruptions to global supply chains, and getting the best freight rate for cargo is more important today than ever before.

Depending on the volume of goods you are sending, using a good customs broker and freight forwarder may be the most efficient way to ship your goods. These companies are experts in documentation, freight rate negotiations and finding the most economical way to get your product to the buyer. Increasingly, you will also find software platforms that perform the same function.

Getting in touch with a few different international shipping companies and checking out a few platforms (Portilius is a pioneer in this field) to compare costs and available services is a good starting point. Along with their expertise in export forms and shipping documentation, many freight forwarders specialise in certain types of shipments.

A good freight forwarder should be able to give you a range of options to find the most cost-efficient rate, but it also pays to become familiar with freight markets so you can get the most competitive rate.

Your overseas buyer will often specify a preferred freight option. This could depend on ease of customs clearance at the port of discharge or the frequency and reliability of sailing. Transhipment is a common feature of liner shipping, and 'hub' ports such as Singapore, Hong Kong and Dubai distribute containerised cargo to other ports by 'feeder' vessels. If you are considering transhipment, make sure you use an efficient transhipment hub so your cargo does not suffer delays.

Incoterms

As you get into the detail of shipping your products, you will also start to encounter shipping terms like FOB, EXW, FCA, CIF and so on. These are all part of Incoterms, a set of internationally-accepted terms spelling out which parties are responsible for various costs and details throughout the shipping process such as freight, insurance, duties, customs clearance and documentation.

Introduced in 1936 and modified since, Incoterms have precise definitions and are critical for the consignment and payment of goods shipped internationally. Incoterms rules are universal and provide clarity and predictability to business around the world. A requirement on every single commercial invoice, they greatly reduce the risk of potentially costly misunderstandings.

- **CFR (Cost and Freight):** The CFR Incoterm means that all charges, including freight up until the intended port of destination, are borne by the seller. However, purchasers should be cautious, as the risk transfers to the purchaser when the goods are loaded on the vessel. Even though the purchaser is not paying for the freight, it carries the risk if anything goes wrong with the goods and so, as a purchaser, it is wise to insure your shipment. All remaining charges at the destination are then settled by the purchaser.
- **CIF (Cost, Insurance and Freight):** This term is the same as CFR only the seller is responsible for the goods and any insurance up until the goods arrive at the intended destination port. Once the goods arrive, the buyer takes on all risks and final associated charges.
- **CIP (Carriage and Insurance Paid To):** Similar to CPT terms, the seller is responsible for making the goods available at a named place of destination. The seller must also procure insurance to cover the goods during transit to the named destination. The buyer is only responsible for any additional transportation and duties and taxes upon arrival.

- **CPT (Carriage Paid To):** For CPT shipments, the seller is responsible for making the goods available at a named place of destination. With these terms, the buyer is responsible for any additional transportation, duties and taxes. The buyer is also responsible for any insurance required during transit.
- **DAP (Delivered At Place):** DAP means the shipment is delivered to a chosen location at the destination. The seller is responsible for all charges up until the goods are delivered to the final location. The buyer is responsible for unloading these goods and any duties and taxes applicable.
- **DDP (Delivered Duty Paid):** DDP terms represent the least cost and risk for the buyer. The seller is responsible for ensuring the goods are delivered to the final destination import cleared. This means the seller takes on all costs and liability for the entire shipment. The buyer is only responsible for unloading goods upon arrival.
- **DPU (Delivered At Place Unloaded):** This requires the seller to deliver the goods to the buyer after they have been unloaded from the transport that has brought them to the destination port. It is the only Incoterms rule that requires the seller to unload goods at the place of destination and it can apply to any – and more than one – mode of transport.
- **EXW (Ex Works):** The Ex Works Incoterm places the lowest level of obligation on the seller in regards to shipping costs and liabilities. The seller makes the goods available at their premises and the buyer must organise all elements of shipping. This includes collection, freight, delivery, duties and taxes. The risk transfers to the buyer when they collect the goods from the named premises and the buyer takes on all costs until final delivery.
- **FAS (Free Alongside Ship):** For FAS shipments the seller makes the goods available alongside the vessel at the named port of shipment and coordinates the export clearance. The seller takes on all origin charges including terminal charges but the buyer pays for loading onto the vessel and all charges thereafter.

- **FCA (Free Carrier):** For FCA shipments, the seller makes the goods available to a carrier specified by the buyer and from here the risks and costs are transferred to the buyer. It is the buyer's responsibility to coordinate the export clearance and bear terminal and loading charges at the port of origin. The buyer must also pay all charges from freight to final delivery and customs charges at the end destination.
- **FOB (Free On Board):** When shipping on FOB terms the seller is responsible for all origin charges, including loading onto the named vessel. Once the goods pass the ship's rail, the risks and costs are transferred to the buyer. The buyer is then responsible for the freight, any insurance required and all charges at the final destination.

To simplify the international contracts and more clearly specify the obligations of buyers and sellers, Incoterms were updated and organised by modes of transport in 2010.

These Incoterms apply to any mode of transport:

- CIP – Carriage and Insurance Paid To
- CPT – Carriage Paid To
- DAP – Delivered at Place
- DDP – Delivered Duty Paid
- DPU – Delivered at Place Unloaded (formerly DAT Delivered at Terminal)
- EXW – Ex Works
- FCA – Free Carrier

These Incoterms apply only to sea and inland waterway transport:

- CFR – Cost and Freight
- CIF – Cost, Insurance, and Freight
- FAS – Free Alongside Ship
- FOB – Free on Board

Knowing your Incoterms and discussing these with your buyer or seller prior to arranging a shipment will avoid any surprises during the shipping process. It is a good idea to speak to your freight forwarder and ask for comparison rates on different terms so you can calculate the best option for your business – before agreeing the terms of sale.

You can find more detailed information on Incoterms at the International Chamber of Commerce (ICC) website, iccwbo.org.

HS Codes

As part of the process to sell internationally, you will also need to know your product's Harmonized System (HS) code. The Harmonized System is an internationally-accepted product classification system administered by the World Customs Organization (WCO), and is the foundation for import and export classification systems used in countries around the world. The HS assigns a six-digit number to each product that is traded internationally. Countries are allowed to add longer codes to the first six digits for further classification.

HS Codes apply to all goods that require international transport, and your product's HS Code is a powerful bit of information. With it, you can use trade data, conduct market research and complete a successful export transaction.

There are thousands of HS Codes, and each code describes specific goods. All customs agencies are able to identify these goods easily using the number associated with the particular commodity.

Take potatoes for example. Fresh or chilled potatoes will be classified as 0701.90, but frozen potatoes will go under the code 0710.10.

Each code has a unique structure as follows:

- A six-digit identification code
- Five thousand commodity groups
- Those groups feature 99 chapters
- The chapters themselves then have 21 sections.

The code is structured and logical and there are approximately 5,300 codes in use. More than 98% of internationally traded goods rely on the HS Code system for their classification.

Who uses HS Codes?

More than 200 countries which are parties to the International Convention on the Harmonized Commodity Description and Coding System use HS Codes. Customs authorities use HS Codes to identify what goods are being shipped and to apply relevant customs duties, taxes and regulations. Governments also use HS Codes to collect global trade statistics and create tariffs. Private companies use the same system to monitor goods, develop and advocate trade policies, collect statistics on traffic and transport and monitor prices.

Where should I use HS Codes in shipping?

When shipping freight, you must use the correct HS Code on each line of your commercial invoice, to ensure that your goods make it through customs seamlessly and without delay, the importer receives the goods faster and you get paid sooner.

Placing the right HS Code on your commercial invoice also means you will pay the correct amount of duty. If you do not include the HS Code on the commercial invoice, the importer risks paying the incorrect duty. You, the exporter, may have to pay interest on any back-payments for incorrect classification, and your goods may even be seized.

Your product's HS Code will tell you if the duty is suspended on any of your products and if any preferential duties rates can be applied on the goods being imported. Australia has free trade agreements with many countries, and using the correct HS Code may allow you to access certain preferential duties arising from those agreements.

An HS Code can also tell you whether tariffs or anti-dumping duties apply to your product. For example, a quick search of HS Code 0203.29.023 reveals that fresh, chilled or frozen swine exported from Australia to Japan is subject to a tariff under the Japan-Australia Economic Partnership Agreement (JAEPA).

You can search HS Codes using the Free Trade Agreement Portal administered by the Department of Foreign Affairs and Trade (DFAT).

How can I find applicable duties and taxes in an overseas market?

You will need the Harmonised Tariff Code (HTC) to search for import tariffs on the Tariff Download Facility on the World Trade Organisation website.

If you do not have the HTC, this can be obtained by contacting the Department of Home Affairs or its equivalent in your home country.

GETTING YOUR EXPORT DOCUMENTATION RIGHT

When sending goods overseas, you will need to complete a suite of 'export documentation' which will enable your goods to traverse international barriers and arrive safely at their destination.

To avoid delays in customs clearance and to comply with documentary letters of credit that specify conditions such as precise product descriptions, packing lists and attestations including quarantine certificates and certificates of origin, you will need to supply documents that are 100% error-free. Electronic documentation has made a complex process much easier, but mistakes can be expensive. The importance of understanding the export documentation process and ensuring that documents are prepared with meticulous accuracy cannot be overstated!

Here is a checklist of the most common export documents you need to include with your shipment when sending goods to another country:

- **Export declaration**. An export declaration is a type of form submitted at the port, providing details about the goods that are bound for export. The export declaration is required each time goods are exported overseas (or outside a customs union) and the document is used by the customs authority to control exports.
- **Commercial invoice**. A document which sets out the buyer, the seller and the terms of the sale. The commercial invoice provides information for the customs authorities, which helps them assess if the goods can move in or out of a country and what, if any, controls are needed. It

also helps them determine duties and taxes. Every shipment must have its own commercial invoice. Your HS Code and Incoterms are among the details that must be included on the commercial invoice.

- **Consignment note.** A document that shows the details of goods that have been sent from a seller to a buyer, and that travels with the goods. It is prepared and signed by the person sending the shipment, and is countersigned by the carrier of the shipment as proof of receipt.
- **Air waybill.** A document that functions as proof of goods being received for shipment by an air carrier – like a ticket for a passenger.
- **Packing list.** A packing list outlines the details of your freight. It typically describes how a shipment is packed and what kind of material is used to pack the goods, the detail of the weight, as well as the dimensions of each item, crate or pallet. Ensuring that a packing list accompanies your shipment can save a significant amount of time and money during an inspection process.
- **Export licence.** An export licence is a government document that authorises or grants permission to conduct a specific export transaction (including the export of technology). Export licences are issued by the appropriate licensing agency after a careful review of the facts surrounding the given export transaction.
- **Certificate of origin.** A certificate of origin (COO) is a declaration that specifies the country or countries your goods were made in. If the country of import or export has a free trade agreement (FTA) with your country, the COO can help you avoid duty charges.
- **Any country-specific free trade agreements or declarations.** You will want to ensure you take advantage of the terms in any free trade agreement between your home country and the country to which you are exporting.

The exact list of documents you need to provide depends on the goods you are shipping, the destination country and export controls – laws and regulations to manage the export of certain items like technology, chemicals or military goods. Sometimes you will need to include additional ones as well.

Seven steps to a successful shipment

1. AGREE INCOTERMS BEFORE YOU GET STARTED

Before you sign an agreement with an international customer, make sure you are clear about who is paying for what and how *risk* will be allocated between you and the customer during the shipping process. You do this by deciding which Incoterm will govern your commercial agreement.

2. GET QUOTES AND CHOOSE YOUR ROUTE

Next, it's time to negotiate quotes for shipping. Here are some things you will need to take into account.

- **Your preferred method of shipping.** As I mentioned above, there are pros and cons to both shipping by air and shipping by sea. Ocean freight is typically less expensive, but air freight is much faster. The best choice for you will depend on how much you are willing to pay, how urgent your shipment is, any contractual obligations you have to your buyer, how much stock you have on hand and what your competitors are offering.
- **What you are shipping.** Knowing the full specification of the product you are shipping is critical to ensure your export goes to plan. For a start, the kind of goods you are shipping will impact on the price of quotes you receive and will affect how they must be transported. For example, some kinds of goods, such as lithium batteries, must be packed in a specific way. Goods containing natural materials must be treated or fumigated, while goods that are classified as dangerous goods may require a permit before they can be shipped.
- **The size of your shipment.** Knowing the size of your shipment (weight, dimensions and volume) is important when requesting a quote and determining your route, because it will influence the cost to ship. It is also important when it comes to deciding what equipment you need to ship your goods.

- **Collection and delivery address.** Once you know how you will ship your goods, you will need to specify exactly where your goods will be shipped to. This will determine the length of the route (including whether transhipment will be required) and the price of quotes you receive.

3. PREPARE YOUR CONSIGNMENT

You have accepted a quote from a shipper and have agreed on pricing. Now it's time to prepare your consignment and make sure your cargo is securely packed. Depending on what you are shipping, this may involve:

- Ensuring you use the correct packaging if you are shipping dangerous goods
- Understanding the import requirements of the destination country
- Selecting the right containers to ship your goods – e.g. if you need refrigerated shipping.

Attention to detail is very important at this stage of the shipping process. You will avoid delays and extra costs if the preparation of your consignment is managed correctly.

4. PREPARE YOUR DOCUMENTATION

Export documentation is detailed and there are several pieces of paper you will need to get ready before you can export. I have listed these above.

5. COMPLETE YOUR SHIPPER'S LETTER OF INSTRUCTION

A Shipper's Letter of Instruction (SLI) is mandatory for all exports and sets out the precise requirements of your shipment from beginning to end. It formalises how your shipment should be handled, and grants authority to your freight forwarder to act as the authorised agent to deal with customs. It is essential to complete this document so that misunderstandings about the shipment do not occur.

6. PAY FOR YOUR SHIPMENT

Once you have booked your shipment, pay for the shipping promptly to ensure goods are not held up on arrival.

7. TRACK YOUR SHIPMENT

You are good to go! Once instructions are given to your forwarder, they will organise the movement of your cargo to meet cut-off times and security requirements of carriers. From here, you can track your cargo online to see when goods will arrive at their intended destination.

CHAPTER 11

GETTING PAID

CHAPTER 11

GETTING PAID

Many companies that I speak to – both in the SME sector and at the big end of town – face challenges with getting paid on time (or at all) when they sell to customers overseas.

In the worst-case scenario, payment problems may force a company out of business in a particular country. This was the case with Australian construction company CIMIC Group Limited (formerly Leightons). It left the UAE market in early 2021 after failing to recover $1.8 billion that it had been owed for more than a decade.

Although most companies will not face a situation this serious as they work or sell abroad, not getting paid is still one of the biggest risks of doing business internationally.

In this chapter, I want to look at the steps you can take to ensure that you get paid, on time and in full.

Background work and research

One way to set yourself up for success as you start selling internationally is to understand the systems, protocols and customs of getting paid in your target market. You should also understand the consequences of not getting paid. Companies doing business overseas are often surprised and unprepared for the very different legislative framework of chasing debt that they encounter there.

As a starting point, research the company you are about to do business with. Look through its portfolio of clients, compare their services and prices, read referrals and testimonials. Do as much research as you can to check the creditworthiness of that company, including running a credit check if one is available in that country.

Also, check the insolvency framework in your target market. Bankruptcy rules are unclear in some jurisdictions, making it relatively easy for a company owner to fold a company to avoid paying a debt.

If you have any doubts about the company simply do not do business with it or at least be prepared to write off the debt if it refuses to pay your invoice later down the line.

Getting paid – what are my options?

To be frank, to succeed in today's global marketplace and win sales against foreign competitors, you will need to offer your clients attractive sales terms supported by appropriate payment methods.

Because getting paid in full and on time is the ultimate goal for each international sale, it is critical that you choose an appropriate payment method that minimises the payment risk while accommodating the client's needs. For you (the exporter), any sale is a gift until you receive payment. For your client (the importer), any payment is a donation until the goods are received. In short, you want to receive payment as soon as possible, preferably as soon as an order is placed or before the goods are sent to the importer. Importers want to receive the goods as soon as possible but to delay payment as long as possible, preferably until after the goods are resold to generate enough income to pay you.

Broadly speaking, there are five primary methods of payment for international transactions. You and your client will need to agree which one works best for both parties.

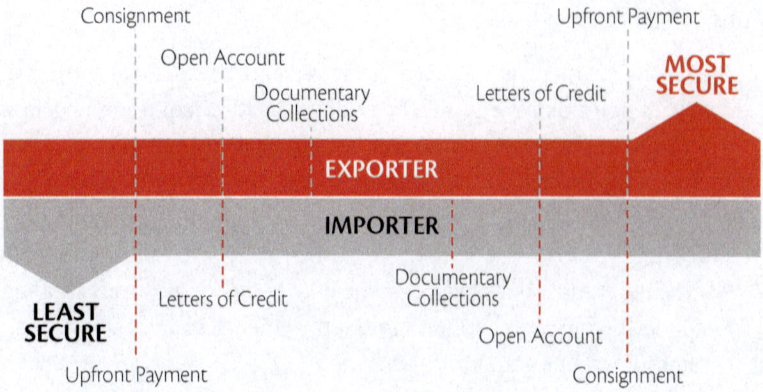

Payment Risk Diagram

UPFRONT PAYMENT

Upfront payment means just what it says: you are paid for your products before delivering your goods to the customer.

Upfront payments enable the seller to avoid credit risk because payment is received before the ownership of the goods is transferred. For international sales, wire transfers and credit cards are the most common upfront payment methods and online escrow services are becoming another upfront option for small international transactions.

However, requiring payment in advance is the least attractive option for the buyer, because it creates unfavourable cash flow. International buyers are also concerned that the goods may not be sent if payment is made in advance. If you insist on upfront payment, you may lose to competitors who offer more attractive payment terms.

Pros

- Least risky form of payment for the seller – you get your money at the time of the sale.
- Upfront payment provides the working capital you need to process the order so there is no strain on your cash flow.
- Simple and clear to transact for the seller.

Cons

- Upfront payment is the least attractive and competitive from the buyer's point of view, as it is the riskiest way for them to do business – they part with their money upfront but have no guarantee you will deliver the goods.
- This method can also tie up a buyer's cash while they are waiting for delivery.
- If the buyer must borrow all or some of the amount, this adds another step to their process and, with interest payments, could increase their total cost to buy your product.
- As a result, few international customers will agree to cash-in-advance purchases, unless the transaction is a small one.

LETTERS OF CREDIT

A Letter of Credit is an important payment method in international trade. It is particularly useful where the buyer and seller do not know each other personally and are separated by distance, differing laws in each country, and different trading customs.

The buyer establishes a credit with his or her bank and pays the bank to render this service. When the seller presents the documents – which are specified in the contract for sale – to the bank, he or she receives payment for the goods from the bank. The seller relies on the credit risk of the bank, rather than the buyer, to receive payment, and if the buyer cannot pay for the purchase, the seller may demand payment from the bank. The bank will examine the seller's demand and if it complies with the terms of the Letter of Credit, will honour the demand.

A Letter of Credit also protects the buyer since no payment obligation arises until the goods have been shipped.

Pros

- The main advantage of using a Letter of Credit is that it can give security to both the seller and the buyer.

- The seller is *reassured* that, providing they present documents in-order and within an agreed timeframe, they will receive their money *in full and on time.*
- A Letter of Credit is one of the *most secure methods of payment* for exporters as long as they meet all the terms and conditions.
- The *risk* of non-payment is transferred from the seller to the bank (or banks).
- When a buyer uses a Letter of Credit they get a *guarantee* that the seller will honour their side of the deal and provide documentary proof of this.

Cons

- Letters of Credit can be expensive. Banks charge for providing them, so it is sensible to weigh up the costs against the security benefits.
- As a seller, you should be aware that you will only receive payment if you keep to the strict terms of the Letter of Credit. You will need to give documentary proof that you have supplied exactly what you contracted to supply.
- Using a Letter of Credit can sometimes cause delays and other administrative problems.

DOCUMENTARY COLLECTIONS

There are two basic types of Documentary Collections: 'documents against payment' and 'documents against acceptance'. For documents against payment, your bank sends a set of shipping documents to a correspondent bank in your customer's market. When your goods arrive at the port of entry, the correspondent bank presents the documents to your customer. The customer pays the bank, receives the shipping documents in exchange, and uses them to release the goods from customs. The correspondent bank then sends the payment to you via your bank.

The process is almost identical for documents against acceptance, except you allow your customer to pay the correspondent bank on some specified future date. At that time, and on the customer's payment, the correspondent bank releases the documents to the customer. You are then paid through your bank.

Documentary Collections do not provide the same level of security as Letters of Credit, but they are less expensive. Unlike the Letters of Credit, for a Documentary Collection the bank acts as a channel for the documents but does not guarantee payment. The bank that has received a Documentary Collection may debit the buyer's account and make payment only if authorised by the buyer.

Pros

- Because the transactions are carried out through banks, with your bank acting as your agent, Documentary Collections carry less risk for you than an Open Account.
- They are also less expensive than Letters of Credit, so they may be a more competitive option if your customer baulks at paying for a Letter of Credit.

Cons

- Unlike Letters of Credit, your bank does not assume liability to pay if your customer will not, or cannot, pay once the goods arrive. It is more secure than an Open Account, but riskier than a Letter of Credit.
- Documentary Collections should therefore be used with extra caution if the market is politically risky or if there is otherwise a risk the buyer will not pay.

OPEN ACCOUNT

Open Account terms mean that you agree to ship your goods to your customer before you get paid. The customer promises to pay within a certain time after receiving the goods, typically within 30 to 180 days.

Pros

- Open Account is a very low-risk option for your customer, as they receive the goods before paying for them.

- Using an Open Account can help you land a sale, but you should be sure that the buyer's credit is good before you agree to it.
- In most markets, offering Open Account terms will make you more competitive, which can increase repeat business and help you build both market share and customer loyalty.

Cons

- The biggest risk with an Open Account is getting paid late, or not getting paid at all.
- If the customer does not pay, you may also incur costs trying to collect on the debt in addition to the loss from unpaid debt itself.
- Simply offering longer payment terms will not necessarily make you the most competitive. It is best to find out what payment terms are most common for your industry in the target market, and remain within them.

CONSIGNMENT

Consignment is a variation of Open Account terms. The seller only receives payment after the goods have been sold by the foreign distributor to the end customer. An international consignment transaction is based on a contractual arrangement in which the foreign distributor receives, manages and sells the goods for the exporter, who retains title to the goods until they are sold.

Exporting on consignment is very risky. The exporter is not guaranteed any payment and its goods are in a foreign country, in the hands of an independent distributor or agent. Selling on consignment can help you become more competitive on the basis of better availability and faster delivery of goods. It can also help to reduce the direct costs of storing and managing inventory. The key to success in exporting on consignment is to partner with a reputable and trustworthy foreign distributor or a third-party logistics provider. You will also need to put in place insurance to cover consigned goods in transit or in possession of a foreign distributor to mitigate the risk of non-payment.

Pros

- Consignment helps you introduce proven products into new sales channels and new or unproven products within current sales channels.
- It potentially ensures long-term business with the buyer.
- Consignment allows you to judge what levels of inventory are turned over in different time periods and can reduce inventory holding costs.

Cons

- Consignment requires you to invest a large amount of money, including shipping costs, into a large amount of new inventory.
- If it does not sell, you risk a loss because you are still the owner of the goods.
- With no monetary risk, the customer may not be motivated to aggressively sell your product.

TO SUM UP

When choosing a payment option for your international business, think about the following questions:

- How much can you trust your buyer?
- Have you established a strong relationship with the client or is this the first transaction with the company?
- How much risk are you prepared to take?
- How much risk is your buyer prepared to take?
- How large is the transaction?
- Can you bargain for more favourable terms with this buyer?

Answering these questions can help you to arrive at the best payment option for your international business, and for the specific transaction that you are dealing with.

Your bank or financial institution can also provide more comprehensive advice about payment options and the relative advantages of each, based on your situation.

OTHER CONSIDERATIONS

Although making sure you choose the right payment option for your international transaction is important, it is not the only thing to consider when it comes to getting paid.

Do not forget Incoterms

As I mentioned in the previous chapter, using the right Incoterms is key to your international contracts. Doing so minimises the risk of any ambiguity in the agreement. Even so, local laws may mean that some Incoterms are not fully effective, and confusion can arise.

A lawyer with expertise in foreign trade can advise you on the detailed requirements of each Incoterm in relation to exports to your target country.

Insurance

When selling to customers overseas, you may want to consider taking out export insurance. You can use credit financing to ensure you get paid as soon as the contract is delivered, and a line of credit can cover a series of contracts, rather than just one.

Other options include arranging insurance privately through an insurance broker, or using a bank or trade finance specialist to both finance your exports and cover you against late payment or default.

Exchange rate risk

It is also wise to take steps to protect yourself against exchange rate risk. Typically, this might be by agreeing the contract in your home currency or by arranging a currency 'hedge' (or possibly a currency option) with your bank or foreign exchange provider.

Monitoring debtors

Once you have started trading, keep an eye on your debtors. Immediately query any deviation from normal trading patterns (e.g. order levels, delivery, settlement, etc). Consider monitoring filings at public registries in countries where your debtors are registered for signs they are in trouble.

CHAPTER 12

INTERNATIONAL MARKETING

CHAPTER 12

INTERNATIONAL MARKETING

In this chapter, I want to explore how to create a marketing message that will work in international markets.

International marketing challenges

Companies encounter a bunch of challenges when it comes to marketing in other countries. Marketing departments often do not know much about the business and cultural context of the international audiences they are trying to reach. Sometimes they are also unsure about what kind of marketing they should be doing, so they either 'copy and paste' – do exactly what has worked for them in their home market – or they take a 'spray and pray' approach by trying a little bit of everything. Neither of these approaches tends to work well.

Finally, they do not track their marketing numbers, measure the results and adjust the strategy accordingly. The upshot is that companies that market like this do not get the results they are hoping for in overseas markets.

Although international marketing operates from the same core marketing principles as domestic marketing, how it works on the ground can be very different. This is because people in different countries have different preferences and expectations.

Take the United States and China for example. Companies the world over dream of winning business in these two superpower economies, and they represent two distinctive kinds of markets: developed Western markets and developing Eastern markets.

The United States and China also differ significantly when it comes to what people care about and what kind of marketing works.

CORE VALUES: PERSONAL APPEAL OR DESIRE TO BE SEEN?

Imagine that Elon Musk and Zhang Zetian (China's youngest female billionaire, also known as Nancy Zhang) attended the same conference. Which one of them is more likely to dress in luxury brands? If you spent a moment researching Musk and Zetian online, you would probably conclude that Zetian would show up in a couture outfit, while Musk would be likely to wear a no-name t-shirt and jacket.

As one of the richest and most famous entrepreneurs in the world, Musk does not need to prove himself or get attention with brand name clothes – he is happy to wear whatever makes him feel comfortable. But as a newcomer to the billionaire scene, Zetian prefers luxury labels because they confirm her financial and social success to anyone who is paying attention.

As you may have guessed, in this illustration Musk represents the US and Zetian represents China. The United States – a developed market – is like Musk. Most consumer goods are affordable and consumers choose products for the benefits that they deliver, not solely on the basis of a brand name. American consumers value how well things work more than what image they project.

China, on the other hand, is a developing market that more closely resembles Zetian. Consumers in China tend to choose brands to project social status, not just for what functionality they can deliver. Savvy international brands are aware of this and have adapted their brand positioning for the Chinese market. For instance, Häagen-Dazs, an American ice-cream brand sold in supermarkets around the world, successfully reinvented itself for the Chinese market as a luxury ice-cream brand sold in boutique stores. In China, the ice-cream sells for more than twice what it does elsewhere. Westerners think of Häagen-Dazs as quality ice-cream, Chinese consumers see it as part of a high-end lifestyle.

PRODUCT SELECTION CRITERIA: INNOVATION OR BRAND CREDIBILITY?

Research also suggests that when it comes to choosing products, US consumers prefer 'innovative' brands, whereas in China 'brand credibility' is the most important factor in choosing one product over another.

This is at least partly because Chinese consumers and manufacturers find themselves in a crisis of trust when it comes to product quality. In the last decade China has been beset by multiple consumer protection scandals – melamine in milk powder, illegal additives in meat, adulterated steamed buns, exploding watermelons primed with growth-promoting chemicals, mercury in baby formula and plastic rice, the list goes on. If food and other consumer products were really compared against the official standards, nearly 50% would be judged substandard.

In a climate of deep mistrust of locally-made products, Chinese consumers look for reassurance when it comes to quality. Large or well-known brands, or those endorsed by word of mouth, tend to do well because fame and social proof conveys quality and reliability. That is why advertising in China tends to highlight brand history or product formula history. For example, all local Chinese cosmetic brands, including recently founded ones, like to claim that their product is based on a traditional Chinese recipe, or that they are partnering with a well-known Western brand.

In the United States, quality is more or less guaranteed, consumer protections are highly evolved and product information is readily available. Consumers believe they can access the information they need. US consumers trust their Food and Drug Administration to protect their safety so they do not look to brand associations or history as proof of product quality. Consequently, product innovation is a key factor for American consumers choosing products, and product advertising tends to focus on newness including new benefits, new packaging or new usage.

REACHING THE MARKET

It is not just how consumers think, what they value and how they choose products that differ between the United States and China – even the mechanics of reaching prospective clients differs.

Online and social media advertising

Whereas Western audiences tend to find online advertising irritating and intrusive, Chinese audiences often welcome well-targeted online advertising as a means of learning about new brands.

And that is not the only difference.

In the United States, consumers use Facebook, Instagram, Twitter and Snapchat, but Chinese audiences have a far greater array of popular and in-country social media channels at their disposal, including WeChat, Sina Weibo, Tencent QQ and Douyin, which is now gaining a global following with its companion site, TikTok. Chinese customers also use industry and topic-specific social media platforms, such as Mafengwo for travel and Keep for health and fitness.

I could go on, but the point I am trying to make here is that you cannot afford to assume that what works in one country will work in another.

Still do not believe me? Here some examples of enormous international marketing blunders made by big companies who assumed that what worked for them at home would work overseas too.

When Coca-Cola first launched in China, its brand name was translated as,

"Bite the Wax Tadpole."

Gerber marketed baby food in Africa with a cute baby on the label, not realising that, in Ethiopia for example, products usually picture the contents of the tin on the label, as many consumers cannot read.

Colgate launched toothpaste in France named 'CUE', without realising a French porn magazine has the same name.

Nike had to recall thousands of products when a decoration intended to resemble fire on the back of sneakers resembled the Arabic script word 'Allah', Arabic for God.

British brand, Electrolux, once marketed its vacuum cleaners in the United States with the tag line:

"Nothing sucks like an Electrolux."

Vicks introduced its cough drops into the German market, not knowing that the German pronunciation of 'v' is 'f', making 'Vicks' slang for sexual intercourse.

International marketing success

If you want to create international marketing that works in the country you have chosen, there are a few things you have to get right.

- **Understand the context.** Your first job as an international marketer is to understand the context for which you are creating marketing. This is the best way of ensuring that you do not fall into the trap of assuming that consumers in the overseas market are similar to consumers in your domestic target and just communicating in a different language.
- **Create a tailored approach.** Once you have got the insights into the cultural and business context of the market, you need to create an approach tailored for that group of people.
- **Research, test and measure.** Finally, with your strategy in place, you need to research the most appropriate channels to use, then test and measure your results.

Aside from a deep understanding of the context, the key here is to reverse engineer your strategy. Work backwards from where you want to be to work out what you need to do. This includes setting specific goals and a timeline for implementation. If you do these things, your odds of getting great traction in your new market are much, much higher.

UNDERSTAND THE CONTEXT

In case you missed it, I will say it once more: to create a marketing strategy that works overseas, it's critical to understand the context – both the cultural context and the business context – in which you are operating. Without context, it's very difficult to market a product in a way that connects with the customer, makes the product interesting and deeply satisfies a need, because these things are culturally determined.

There are a lot of misconceptions in this space. I hear people saying things like:

> *"We don't need to do a bunch of contextual research for overseas markets. We have a great product and our company has been very successful at our home, so we can just keep on doing what we have done well... and it'll work."*

But that is rarely the case. When you cross national borders, you cross cultural borders as well. In some cases, you may find that you are not even competing in the same category as you were in your home market. Your competition set could be broader, or you might be speaking to a different user base.

In a large company context, mapping out a marketing strategy for a new country is often a massive exercise which costs millions of dollars. Big companies look at things like where the opportunities are, segmentation and 'need gaps'. Once they have segmented the market, they cherry-pick the one or two segments where they believe they can make a real impact. They review the product, as well as brand naming and packaging, because different nationalities see design differently. Shopper research – how people buy a product, how often they buy and how they use the product – is also a focus. Finally, large companies track how people respond to their advertising campaigns and adjust their strategy accordingly.

In a small company, there is just not the budget or resources to do investigation and research to the same scale. But, by looking at four key areas, you can still get a good understanding of the cultural and business context you will be operating in and what kind of marketing is likely to work.

Cultural context

One of the simplest ways that you can become familiar with the general and business culture of the country you plan to sell to is by opening a culture file. Start collecting information on the culture of your target market and research as many aspects of your target culture as you can including:

- History
- Location
- Ethnic make-up
- Religions
- Society and culture
  - Values
  - Etiquette and customs
  - Meeting and greeting
  - Dining
  - Giving gifts
  - National holidays and festivals
  - Arts and culture
  - Other traditions
- Business etiquette and protocol
  - Building relationships and communication
  - Business meetings and negotiation
  - Business card etiquette.

Competitive landscape

As you prepare to enter a new target market, you need to get a sense of the competitive landscape. You can do this by looking at rivals operating in the same geography. Understanding what they are doing and what they have put into the market – both in terms of product and marketing – reveals information about the market itself.

Specifically, look at competitor marketing. Your competitors' journeys – what they did and how they entered the market – can reveal a lot about the consumers and the customers in that country. Competitor marketing also tells you about how competitors are positioning themselves in the market, and how that compares with how they position themselves at home – useful information that you can draw on as you create your own strategy.

Consumption culture

You will also need to get a handle on consumption culture in your target market – how people buy and use products, especially around your product category.

For example, consumers in countries like the US and Australia that rank high on individualism – where people strive to stand out from the crowd and think primarily of themselves when buying products – tend to be far more likely to shop in various channels (retail stores, online, and catalogue) and return items that do not meet their expectations. Because they are generally more interested in chasing the latest trend than staying true to a particular brand, they hop from store to store (or website to website) to find the best deal.

By contrast, in collectivist countries such as Portugal, Mexico and Turkey, people tend to follow the wisdom of crowds and value a product or brand's long-term reputation, rather than its novelty. Consumers in these countries typically buy things for their families rather than just for themselves. They are more likely to buy multiple items from different departments of a trusted retailer, and they like to see or feel the products in person, avoiding catalogues and the internet. They share many characteristics with consumers in 'indulgent' societies, usually in North and South America and Western Europe, where consumers also seek the instant gratification of experiencing or testing an item in a store and enjoy the freedom of trying out a wide range of products.

It is also important to understand how your end users use your product in their home or business. For example, Minnow Designs, an Australian brand that sells swimmable shoes for babies and children as outdoor-wear in Australia, discovered that parents in other countries are buying the soft but durable shoes for indoor wear.

If you are using a distributor or agent, do not leave this step to your in-country partner. Understanding how your client uses your product in an overseas market will give you a tremendous advantage in your conversations with your partner. It also allows you to keep control over your brand, because you demonstrate to the partner that you know your customers.

Concept evaluation

Lastly, evaluate the concept that you are putting into the market. Set up a focus group with potential clients in your new geography to ask questions about your product and marketing concept and how these would work for them, to see if your assumptions about the concept and marketing message match reality.

CREATE A TAILORED APPROACH

You have understood the context, now it's time to decide on a marketing approach for your new market. That decision should be based on what kind of marketing is most likely to get traction for you in that country. You need to get results rapidly, and you need to find out quickly whether your carefully laid plans are going to bear fruit. In other words, you are looking for traction – qualitative evidence of customer demand.

Traction is a sign that your business is going to take off in the new market that you are entering. It is obvious in your core metrics. Leads are pouring in, your monthly transactions are increasing; if you are an IP provider, your monthly downloads are skyrocketing.

As you develop traction, you get a steady stream of cold customers. It is through these people that you can really find out whether the market is taking to your product or not, and if not, what features are missing or which parts of the experience are broken.

- Pursuing traction helps you, because you can use the information that you get from it to adjust your international strategy.
- Traction gets you data about the messages that resonate with your international customers, confirms which niche or market segment you should focus on first, which customers will be easiest to acquire and what distribution roadblocks you might run into.

The next step in creating an international marketing strategy that flies is to choose the right traction channel – a marketing channel that can deliver real customer growth.

Choose some channels

When you are starting out in a new market, it is wise to choose just one or two channels to focus your international marketing efforts on. Each channel you open uses resources and focus. If you can find one that works, stick to it. Less is more, particularly at the beginning.

Gabriel Weinberg and Justin Mares, who wrote the book *Traction: How Any Startup Can Achieve Explosive Customer Growth*, discovered two common themes when it comes to selecting traction channels. Firstly, we stick with what we know... but we should not. Most people only consider using traction channels they are familiar with, or they think they should be using because of their type of product or company. Too many companies focus on the same channels and ignore other ways to get traction, but the most underutilised channels in an industry are often the most promising ones.

Secondly, you will not get proof until you try. Mares and Weinberg's research highlighted that although founders and marketers often think they know which channels will be successful, they are often wrong. It is hard to predict which traction channels will work best and you will not know until you start running tests.

Run some tests

Before you nail down which marketing channels you are going to use in your new international market, you should run some tests, using several channels that you think have promise. The goal is to answer the following questions in broad terms:

- How much will it cost to acquire customers through this channel?
- How many customers are available through this channel?
- Are the customers that you are getting through this channel the kind of customers that you want right now?

It is easy to mess up this step by prematurely scaling up your marketing efforts. I have seen companies throw away hundreds of thousands of dollars, trying to scale up a marketing strategy that wasn't the right one. Keep in mind that when testing, you are not trying to get a lot of traction in that channel *just yet*. Instead, you are simply trying to determine if this is a channel that *could* move the needle for your company as it goes into a new international market. Your main consideration at this point is speed – to get data and prove your assumptions.

In the testing phase, design smaller-scale tests that do not require much upfront cost or effort. For example, run four Facebook ads rather than 40. You should be able to get a rough idea of a channel's effectiveness with a maximum of $1,000 and a month at a time. Often it will be cheaper and shorter. Trade shows in international markets are a bit of an exception to the rule, as they become expensive quickly once you include travel, accommodation and exhibition costs.

How marketers mess up

Marketers often mess up by continuing with distracting marketing efforts in several channels rather than focusing on just one. Imagine that you ran tests in three channels: search engine marketing, trade shows and public relations. Search engine marketing was the most promising so you decided to focus on it and make it your core channel. However, your trade show and publicity tests were also successful, albeit much less so. There is a natural tendency to do more trade shows and PR, because you know that they will work to some degree. But this is a mistake, because it disperses your energy and focus, and stops you performing at maximum capacity in the core channel you have chosen. It is smarter to really focus on one channel and become an expert in it, uncovering new strategies and tactics within it. Wait until you have consolidated your success in one channel, before you start looking at others.

If, after testing, no channel seems promising, you should repeat the whole process again. The good news is that you now have the data from the tests you have already run, which will tell you what types of messaging are or are not resonating with customers. If you go through the process several times and no channel seems promising, then your offering may require more tweaking.

Research, test and measure

We have talked about understanding the business and cultural context and about choosing a marketing channel that makes an impact. Now look at how we can use reverse engineering to break things down even further, into a series of targets and steps.

QUANT-BASED MARKETING

Quant-based marketing is all about working backwards. Instead of starting with a big zero playing on your mind, start at the solution and map your plan back from there.

Think of it as a road trip – you start with a set destination in mind and then plan your route to get there. You do not get in your car and start driving in the hope that you will magically end up where you wanted to be.

We can work through this process in seven steps:

Step 1 – Define a Traction Goal

Before you go about getting traction overseas, you need to know what traction means for your company. You need to set a Traction Goal. You should figure out what this goal means in terms of hard numbers.

You find your Traction Goal by asking:

- How many customers do we need and at what growth rate?
- By when do we need this outcome?

You should always have an explicit Traction Goal you are working towards. This could be 1,000 paying customers, 100 new customers monthly, or 10% of your new market. The right goal is highly dependent on your business.

Make sure it aligns with your company strategy. You want a goal where hitting the mark would change things significantly for your company. Perhaps you would be profitable in your new market, or become the market leader.

The importance of choosing the right Traction Goal cannot be overstated. Are you going for growth, or profitability, or something in between? If you need to raise money in a certain timeframe, what do you need to do so? These are the types of questions that help you determine the right Traction Goal.

Once your Traction Goal is defined, you can work backwards and set clear quantitative and time-based traction sub-goals, such as reaching 100 clients by next quarter or 20% monthly growth.

Step 2 – Choose a timeframe

Without a timeframe, there is no sense of urgency to achieve your goal, and it can be hard to work out whether you are on track or lagging.

Saying *"We need $10,000 per month someday"* will not work. But if you anchor it within a timeframe, like *"We need $10,000 per month in three months"*, it creates urgency. You are instantly set in motion and ready to start working towards your goal.

One hundred new customers in three months. Now that sounds like a real goal, right? You could even break it down further to 16 new customers per week.

Step 3 – Set up tracking

Once you have a clear Traction Goal in mind, you can start building a strategy to achieve it.

A simple way to do this is by using a quant-based marketing spreadsheet to plan, track and measure all of your marketing activity. The most important part here is putting a framework in place to enable your success.

Step 4 – Choose your channels

With your tracking framework ready to go, it's time to start thinking about your sources and where your customers are going to come from.

There are thousands of tactics and channels you can use as a part of your marketing strategy, and this step is all about narrowing them down and choosing specific sources to focus on to achieve your goal.

If you have run some initial tests and demonstrated which channels are likely to be effective in your target market, you can go ahead and put the most promising channel (or two, at most) that you selected into the framework.

Step 5 – Set up your channel targets

With your channels in place, it's time to set your targets for each source.

This is one of the most important parts of your strategy. Once you have launched your campaign for each source, these targets will give you something to measure against and figure out what is working, what is not and where you need to adjust.

So, how do you go about setting targets for your sources?

When it comes to online traffic, you can often find benchmarks by using tools like Similarweb or Semrush, particularly if you are targeting well-known sites.

CTR (click-through rate) and Conversion % is a little harder to gauge. Not all publications will share CTRs and Conversion % for previous advertisers. The point is not about CTR or conversion but what outcomes you expect to get from the source. You may have to search for some case studies and read up about others' experiences with each publication you are targeting.

There are far more benchmarks out there for advertising platforms like Facebook and Google AdWords. For example, WordStream found that the average CTR on AdWords paid search ads is about 2%. So, if AdWords is part of your strategy, you will likely want to aim for around 2% CTR.

When setting your targets, the trick is to use your best guess as a starting point. The goal is to help you prioritise your marketing activities and then to test and measure as you go.

Step 6 – Smaller slices

Now you have set your sources and targets, the next step is to break down these targets into smaller, time-focused goals and create a timeline.

No matter what timeframe you are working with, break it down into smaller, more achievable chunks. If your timeframe is three months, set monthly targets. If it's three weeks, break it down into weekly targets.

Why should you do this?

Aside from making your goals feel more achievable, it's also highly motivating to tick off the smaller goals on route to achieving your overall target.

With each of your sources, take your overall targets and break them down into more manageable chunks that fit within your timeframe.

For instance, you could breakdown a goal of 1,000 new users from Facebook ads as follows:

- Week 1: 50 users
- Week 2: 100 users
- Week 3: 250 users
- Week 4: 500 users.

With this approach, you are not heading into Week 1 thinking *'I have to get 1,000 users.'* You are setting yourself a smaller goal and creating time to experiment and learn what works.

After the first week, you can begin to make tweaks and start scaling as you progress and get more familiar with how to drive the best results from each source.

Step 7 – Track your progress

You have now reverse engineered your international marketing strategy and should be all set to get the ball rolling. But like any form of great marketing, this is not something you can set and forget.

You need to be constantly measuring and iterating to achieve your goals. Once you go live, some sources might work right off the bat, especially those you may be a little more experienced with. But you will not hit a homerun with every source you try, and that is perfectly fine. I like to check back against my assumptions monthly. From there I take the ones performing and see if I can double them, the ones underperforming I will generally kill, immediately.

TIP Diarise a weekly metrics meeting with your team. Go through the numbers, talk about what is working, what is not working and why. Agree on changes to the strategy, assign roles then go ahead and implement.

The most important thing is to ensure you are on track to hit your end goal. The first few weeks or months of your strategy will likely feature a lot of experimentation and testing until you find what works.

This is why measuring your results is key – in a format that is easy to read. It's so you can spot where you need to adjust your plan.

If a source is underperforming, and you have tried multiple tests to get to the bottom of why that is, you can drop it and replace it with another source.

Likewise, if a source begins to perform exceedingly well, you should double down your resources there to maximise your growth.

What if I already have a great marketing strategy?

If you already have a great strategy that is getting results at home or in another market, you may not need to start from scratch. One option is to take the core of the existing strategy and customise it for your new markets. The caveat here is that you still need to do the work to understand the new geography, so you can fit what you already have into the new market's landscape.

CHAPTER 13 FIGURING OUT THE RULES

CHAPTER 13

FIGURING OUT THE RULES

Welcome to the 'why', 'what' and 'how' of the regulatory challenges that come up in an international expansion. Specific regulations vary from country to country and from industry to industry so I will talk in very general terms about the regulatory environments that you may have to comply with overseas, the kinds of risks you may face, and the potential impact on your business.

I will also show you how to minimise the risks from regulatory issues, so that you avoid unpleasant surprises. Digging into rules and regulations might sound deadly dull, but this is a complex and crucial area for anyone planning to operate a business internationally.

Top mistakes that people make in this space include:

- **Insufficient research** – they do not verify information and triangulate it with other sources.
- **Rely on the black and white** – they focus too much on the written laws and regulations and fail to take account of 'soft' law, how regulations are enforced, or the prevailing political mood and trends.
- **Insufficient monitoring** – they fail to keep abreast of changes and the rise of new trends or issues.

The way around these mistakes is to:

- **Do your homework** – consult with as wide a range of people as possible. Test and verify the information and insights you get. This does not have to be expensive or time consuming and can be combined with other activities.
- **Appreciate the nuance** – look at how regulations are made and enforced, and the agenda behind the regulations.
- **Set up an early warning system** – build relationships and goodwill early on.

Understanding the context

Just as with choosing a market, understanding your ideal international client, or creating marketing that works overseas, understanding the context is important when it comes to regulatory frameworks. The goal is to get as much knowledge as you can, in the shortest amount of time and for the least cost. You can do this by talking to people. It does not have to be an expensive activity, as many of them are people you would be talking to anyway. It is about getting behind the news headlines and really understanding what is going on in your sector and the wider context.

As you start going global, you will probably engage a local, in-country lawyer or accountant to help you. These are fantastic people to tap for information and, if they are worth their salt, they should be happy to talk through what they think about the local political situation and how things are developing in the regulatory environment.

Other good sources of local information could be your embassy in the country you are trying to enter. Commercial teams at embassies are often good to talk to, because they have been doing business in the country a long time and know how things develop, how things work and how decisions are made.

In terms of where to look to get this information, the following places should be initial ports of call:

- Publicly available information including press, media and social media
- Local lawyer

- Embassy
- Chambers of commerce
- Trade associations
- Business networking organisations

One of the first steps is to map out who your stakeholders are. You can do this under three headings.

WHO INFLUENCES OR REGULATES THE ENVIRONMENT?

Under this first category, you are trying to identify everyone who will have some kind influence on the shape of the business environment you are going into. Try to find out:

- What minister or ministries are responsible for regulating your area in the new market? It may be more than one if your product or your service crosses boundaries and does not fit neatly into one box.
- Is there a federal system in the state government or the municipal government in the city where you are going to be operating? Will you need to comply with more than one tier of regulation?
- Within the ministry or ministries, who are the key officials or key departments that you will need to deal with?
- If there is an independent regulator, who are they?

WHO SHAPES OR SHARES YOUR SUCCESS?

The second set of stakeholders are those who shape or share your success.

As I already mentioned, your local lawyer or accountant, your partners, suppliers and staff – those who benefit from your success – are all good sources of information and insight into what is happening.

WHO ARE THE COMMUNICATORS?

The third set of stakeholders is 'communicators'. These are the people who you can communicate with, those who can give you insights, and also help influence the other two groups. This group specifically includes the trade press in your industry and may also include your embassy or chambers of commerce.

Understanding the process

Another area to investigate is how regulations are made and what the process is. Is it transparent and open? Are you able – either individually or through a business group or network – to influence the regulations or put your point of view across about what reforms or changes are needed?

You also need to understand how regulations are enforced, who is responsible for enforcing them, whether enforcement is strict and how independent the regulator is.

Triangulate your information

Understanding the regulatory environment is about doing proper detective work and it is a good idea to cross-check your information. Do not just rely on one or two sources or seemingly reliable pieces of information; try and broaden this out so that you can triangulate information and understand the broader agenda of the regulator or relevant government department. Government officials have particular agendas which are wider than your business area, and you should compare what you hear from government sources with what the embassy says, what the chamber of commerce says, what you read in the press, and what you pick up at business networking events.

Do not make the mistake of becoming too reliant on the same few trusted people, as it can lead you to putting less emphasis on some of the downside risks, or blind you to things coming out of left field.

Finding the answers to these questions is a great place to start:

- What ministry or other government agencies regulate your sector?
- Is there an independent regulator?

- How competent is the regulator?
- Are the regulations clear?
- When was the last update?
- What is the process for changing regulations?
- To what extent will you be able to influence implementation or changes?
- What are the trends in your sector?

Your product

As well as understanding the general regulatory environment, you will also need to comply with regulations relating to actual products and services. Questions to ask yourself when it comes to your product in a new international market include:

- What standards does it have to meet?
- What licences are required?
- Does it comply with health and safety laws?
- What are the packaging requirements?
- Is there anything about how it interacts with the local language which will not work?
- Are there country-specific transport and storage requirements?

A PRODUCT COMPLIANCE NIGHTMARE

Several years ago, I worked with a small Australian company that sold designer homewares wholesale to retailers in the United States. Its key channel into international markets was a long-standing, stable relationship with a major American retailer.

The company was on the cusp of expanding its operations to Japan when it was sued under California's Proposition 65, also called the *Safe Drinking Water and Toxic Enforcement Act*. The law – which is intended to help Californians make informed decisions about protecting themselves from chemicals that could cause cancer, birth defects or other reproductive harm – requires companies to include warning labels on products that contain even trace amounts of the chemicals or substances on the Proposition 65 List.

My client had been completely unaware of Proposition 65 and none of its products sold in California carried the appropriate warning label. Shortly after the lawsuit popped up, the major retailer dropped the company as a supplier, dramatically reducing cash flow and throwing all areas of the business into disarray. Although the company held on by a thread and kept trading, its international plans were permanently shelved.

As that company's experience illustrates, it is vitally important that you familiarise yourself with compliance obligations relating to your product, and that you fulfil them!

Establishing a presence

Not everyone will need to set up a presence in-market right away, but when you do, here are some of the regulatory considerations you will need to take into account:

- How do we register a company and what form should it take?
- Do we need a partner?
- What name and logos can we use?
- Can foreigners own land?
- Will the banking system work the way we want it to?

Not so long ago, I worked with a company to set up offshore operations and banking in a Pacific jurisdiction. It was the company's first real foray into international markets and they had not thought carefully through what banking facilities they needed, and which ones were merely nice to have. They were frustrated to discover that the only bank in the jurisdiction which would accept them as a client had far less sophisticated facilities than they were accustomed to at home.

Hiring and firing

When you start up in a new market, you may not have any staff. However, as you grow, you may need a team on the ground, whether these are sales representatives, consultants, office or warehouse managers. Here are some questions to ask yourself:

- What are the regulations concerning employing staff e.g. need to provide minimum conditions?
- What is the minimum wage?
- Are there compulsory pension, health or other costs?
- Are there any workforce localisation policies?
- What are the regulations for work permits for expatriates?
- How easy is it to fire staff?

In Indonesia, for example, hiring expatriate workers is difficult. Government policy requires that domestic or foreign companies operating in Indonesia should not hire an expatriate to do a job that can be carried out by an Indonesian.

For the Indonesian government to accept a company's application for the employment of an expatriate, the employing company must:

- Justify why the position needs to be filled by an expatriate
- Demonstrate that the expat has the proper educational background
- Respond to the questions of the Ministry of Manpower at an interview
- Show that there is an open slot in the company's manpower plan, previously approved by the Ministry of Manpower.

If these requirements (and others) are satisfied, then the expatriate can be issued a work permit. After the work permit is approved, the company can apply for a semi-resident visa for the new employee.

Employers of expatriates are required to implement training programs for Indonesian employees and it is necessary for foreign companies to have an Indonesian national employed as a counterpart to every expatriate employee.

In addition to the applications and bureaucratic hassles of hiring foreigners, the Ministry of Manpower imposes a tax of $1,200 on every foreign employee hired. The tax is applied to training programs to upskill Indonesians.

Indonesia's strict labour laws, which make termination of employees extremely difficult, is another challenge for employers, particularly foreign companies that do not maintain a full human resource capacity in the country.

China is another case in point. Officially, there is no regulation explicitly placing quotas on the number of expats a company can hire. However, local government agencies – often the municipal Human Resources and Social Security Bureau – have the authority to decide on applications for hiring foreign employees. In practice, these agencies have a habit of refusing applications for foreign employees over a certain limit. The guidelines are not published or explicitly revealed through any channels.

Anecdotal evidence from firms on the ground suggests that when assessing whether it is necessary for a company to hire foreigners, and if so, how many, the government considers things like the applicant's business scope and size, registered capital and internal structure, as well as the specific position in question. For example, a company with little registered capital wanting to hire a large number of foreigners is likely to see its application refused.

Companies may directly enquire with the relevant authorities, providing details such as their registered capital and target industry, to get an understanding of how many foreigners they will likely be allowed to hire, or engage with a local accountant, lawyer or business consultant, to assist them in sourcing this information.

Operations

In addition to product, establishment and labour relations regulations, you will need to bear in mind regulations that may affect your ability to import products into a market, such as:

- Health and safety regulations
- Customs regulations
- Tax regulations, including value added taxes (VAT, GST, state taxes)
- Local content regulations
- The need to comply with an inspection regime.

At times, these regulations can seem quirky. In the UAE, for example, livestock are inspected upon arrival. Agricultural pesticides may only be imported by a registered importer holding a valid import licence, and imports of pharmaceutical products are subject to specific transport regulations.

In India, live animals, plants, and parts of plants must come with health certificates issued by an approved authority in the country of origin. Plants can only be imported through ports where fumigation and inspection facilities are available and fruit, vegetables and all foodstuffs must be inspected on arrival. Food quality and purity are subject to strict national and state regulations. These also cover the use of preservatives, colouring matter, artificial sweeteners, and containers and their marking and labelling.

CHAPTER 14 PROTECTING YOUR INTELLECTUAL PROPERTY

CHAPTER 14

PROTECTING YOUR INTELLECTUAL PROPERTY

Whether you are setting up shop in a new country, or just selling your stuff there, you will need a strategy for managing your intellectual property (IP) as you expand internationally.

IP is the property of your mind. It can be a totally new concept or invention, an innovative design, a distinctive brand, or a combination of all three.

Whatever form your IP takes, it is one of your most important business assets – it's what differentiates you from your competitors, and while it is an intangible asset, it has a very tangible value. That is why you should consider protecting it from being used by other individuals or businesses.

A lot of business owners do not know what IP they should protect. All businesses have IP, but many business owners have never stopped to think through, in detail, what that IP is and which bits of it they need to protect at home and in international markets.

Many business owners are also unfamiliar with the law that applies to taking their IP overseas, so they do not know what options are available. For example, many do not realise that even if they protect their IP in their home market, this provides no protection beyond domestic shores – potentially providing third parties with the opportunity to copy and sell a product in other jurisdictions. Even fewer have a strategy in place for protecting their IP abroad.

There are two big risks here:

- You have your IP infringed
- You infringe someone else's IP without realising it.

A couple of quick examples

If you are selling in an offshore market without protection, there is nothing to stop someone from reverse engineering and copying your product – right down to its packaging and logo. Or they could package something so that it looks very similar to your product – not quite close enough to be considered as passing off as your product or trademark, but close enough to damage your reputation.

For example, a small Dutch company produced additives in China under the name Roi Jaguar. Their Chinese general manager was tasked with making sure that the brand was protected in accordance with Chinese law. He eventually left the company and, soon after, a similar product called Roi Lynx appeared on the Indian market.

The Dutch company discovered that after quitting the job, its former general manager had begun competing against it with similar products. It also found out that he had registered the trademarks of the company in China in his own name instead of under the name of the Dutch company.

The situation escalated after the former manager claimed that the Dutch company owed him money – a claim it refuted. The former general manager then went to the local Authority of Industry and Commerce (AIC) and showed them Roi Jaguar's trademark certificate, which was registered in his name. AIC confiscated the Dutch company's products, which carried the name Roi Jaguar and had infringed the Chinese trademark certificate.

As the former general manager owned Roi Jaguar's Chinese trademark registration, he was also able to force the Dutch company to close down its business with regard to the Roi Jaguar brand.

The company took action against the former general manager and was able to prove that the trademark registration had been carried out in bad faith because the general manager had a pre-existing relationship with the company. The company filed for a trademark cancellation on the grounds of bad faith and then applied for the trademark itself, registering the wordmark, logo and the Chinese character name of its product.

On the other hand, you might have protected your IP in your home country, but you may not know if someone else has already protected that same IP in their country. You may not know that you are actually infringing on someone else's rights until you seek protection for your own IP and find that you cannot get it because it conflicts with someone else's registration. Or, you may get a nasty letter from a foreign-based law firm, telling you that you are infringing on their client's rights. This can be the result of a genuine situation where that trademark was already in use in that market for the same or different purposes. However, it's not unusual for this to be a result of IP squatting, where a third party registers their right to the IP with the hope of selling it for financial gain later on.

Know what IP to protect

In any business there will be a range of IP that you can protect. This includes:

- Inventions
- Symbols
- Names and images
- Designs
- Confidential information
- Written works
- Architectural design
- Media
- Advertisements
- Computer programs
- Databases
- Films
- Musical compositions
- Paintings
- Drawings
- Photographs, sculpture, architecture
- Maps and technical drawings

All these things are covered by IP rights which are like any other property right. IP rights allow creators or owners of patents, trademarks or copyrighted works to benefit from their own work or investment in a creation.

These rights are outlined in Article 27 of the Universal Declaration of Human Rights, which provides for the right to benefit from the protection of moral and material interests resulting from authorship of scientific, literary or artistic productions.

TRADEMARKS

A trademark typically protects brand names and logos used on goods and services.

Examples of world-famous trademarks include:

- The word 'Nike' with its 'swoosh' logo
- The word 'McDonalds' with its 'golden arches' logo.

A trademark can include words, letters, names, phrases, colours, symbols, pictures, signatures, shapes, scents, sounds or even a moving image. A trademark basically represents a business' brand in a sign.

Trademark protection ensures that the owners of marks have the exclusive right to use them to identify goods or services, or to authorise others to use them in return for payment. The period of protection varies, but a trademark can be renewed indefinitely.

DESIGNS

Design is the shape, configuration, pattern and ornamentation of a product – essentially, what it looks like, not what it does. A design may consist of three-dimensional features such as the shape or surface of an article, or two-dimensional features such as patterns, lines or colours.

In general, three-dimensional works that are one-off pieces will be protected under copyright law. Copyright protection applies automatically when the work is created, whether it is a drawing, sculpture, model of a house or other three-dimensional 'work'.

PATENTS

A patent is an exclusive right granted for an invention – a product or process that provides a new way of doing something, or that offers a new technical solution to a problem. A patent provides patent owners with protection for their inventions. Protection is granted for a limited period, generally 20 years. Some famous Australian examples of inventions that have been patented include the Cochlear implant, HEGS Pegs, My Flight Hammock and the Hills Hoist clothesline.

COPYRIGHT

Copyright laws grant authors, artists and other creators protection for their literary and artistic creations, generally referred to as 'works'. A closely associated field is 'related rights' or rights related to copyright that encompass rights similar or identical to those of copyright, although sometimes more limited and of shorter duration.

Works covered by copyright include, but are not limited to, novels, poems, plays, reference works, newspapers, advertisements, computer programs, databases, films, musical compositions, choreography, paintings, drawings, photographs, sculpture, architecture, maps and technical drawings.

OTHER TYPES OF IP

Other types of IP exist to protect trade secrets and information not in the public domain. These include plant breeders' rights to protect new varieties of plants, and circuit layout rights to protect original layout designs for integrated circuits and computer chips.

Protecting your brand

The most effective way for you to protect your brand name and other elements of your brand identity (such as logos and taglines) is to register a trademark.

A common misconception among business owners is that business name and domain name registrations are sufficient to protect their brand name. The reality is that these are administrative steps that do not offer any ownership or protection of the brand name itself.

It is smart to register your brand name and other brand identifiers as a trademark to ensure these are protected as you operate overseas.

The caveat here is that if you are just starting out and your brand is not well established, or you think that you might change your brand, the brand identity might not be worth a lot. It is a good idea to weigh the value of your brand against the cost of trademarking.

The World Intellectual Property Organisation's (WIPO) international cost calculator is https://www.wipo.int/madrid/en/fees/calculator.jsp.

PROTECT YOUR MOBILE APP

Protecting your mobile applications begins with protection of the name, logo, or slogan through trademark law.

Protecting the app's brand helps app developers to better control consumer perception of the app by distinguishing the developer's app from other apps available on the market.

A protectable trademark gives developers an exclusive right to use the mark on, or in connection with, the goods or services provided by the app.

It is important, however, for the developer to ensure that the name, logo or slogan chosen for the app does not infringe another app owner's right in a mark, so the developer must follow proper clearance procedures before choosing a brand.

HOW DO I PROTECT MY TRADEMARK OVERSEAS?

You can seek to protect your trademark in a number of ways:

- You can file directly in the country or countries to which you wish to export
- You can file an application under the Madrid Protocol to cover multiple countries

Trademark registration

Before registering your trademark overseas, you must first take the following steps in your home territory:

- First, an application for registration of a trademark must be filed with the appropriate national trademark office.
- The application must contain a clear reproduction of the sign filed for registration, including any colours, forms or three-dimensional features.
- It must also contain a list of the goods or services to which the sign would apply.
- The sign that is being trademarked must fulfil certain conditions to be protected as a trademark or other type of mark. The two main requirements are:
  - the trademark is distinctive
  - there are no other similar trademarks pending or registered for the same or similar goods or services on the trademarks register (citations).

Registration protects your trademark by:

- Giving you the exclusive right to use the trademark in the jurisdiction it is registered in, for the goods or services for which the trademark is registered.
- Preventing other people from using your trademark or a trademark which is too similar in the same category of goods or services.
- Conferring the right to display the ® symbol next to your trademark to communicate a professional brand image and warn others of the registration rights.
- Protecting the goodwill and reputation that a business builds up over time.
- Creating a valuable asset – once registered, a trademark becomes an asset that can be sold or licensed to others.

Trademark protection is legally enforced by courts that, in most systems, have the authority to stop trademark infringement.

TIP Registering a social media account, business name, company name or domain name (at home or abroad) is not sufficient to protect your brand. Trademark registration is the most effective form of protection for a business' brand.

The Madrid Protocol

For countries that are part of the Madrid Protocol, you may file a single application to seek protection in these countries of interest and pay a single application fee. Note, the application through the Madrid Protocol must be based on your prior – home country – application or registration (the basic trademark).

The Madrid Protocol is a treaty that provides international registration of a trademark. It is administered by the International Bureau of WIPO in Geneva. It facilitates filing of trademark applications in a number of countries in one application.

All requests for protection in Madrid Protocol member countries are examined according to the trademark legislation and laws existing in the designated countries. You may want to get the advice of an IP professional who is familiar with the details of each country.

WIPO provides a full list of member countries that an international application can cover.

Conversely, the Madrid Protocol also allows trademark owners overseas to designate a home market in their international applications. This means that international traders could have trademarks similar to yours that are operational in your domestic market. You should check databases to make sure there are no crossovers.

Requirements to apply for an international trademark are:

- You must have an application and/or a registration in your home country on which to base your application
- You must meet entitlement requirements within that country
- The mark on the international application must be identical to that contained on the original application/registration
- The goods and services in your international application must be covered by the claims in the original application/registration
- The applicant on the international application must also be the applicant on the original application/registration.

Pros

- It is easy and cost effective, with lower fees than applying directly in each country
- International trademark registrations last for 10 years.

Cons

- Fees are due up front
- It can be difficult to determine the status of the mark in the national offices
- The international registration depends on the survival of the basic trademark for five years from the date of application – this can be a problem if your basic mark is unable to be registered
- A number of significant markets, including Canada, Hong Kong and South Africa, are not members of the Madrid Protocol, and do not offer protection under this system – this can be a problem if you are planning to export to these countries
- If there are any objections to the registration, applicants will need to appoint local counsel, which increases the cost of this approach.

Use it or lose it

In some jurisdictions, including Australia and China, if your registered trademark is unused for three consecutive years, you risk having it removed from the register – which means you could lose your exclusive rights to use it.

Protecting the 'look' of your product

If your product relies on its design – or the design of its packaging – to differentiate it in the marketplace, you may consider protecting this design so that you have the exclusive right to prevent others from using it commercially, such as licensing or selling it. You can do this by registering the design and paying the relevant fees.

Design registration does not protect the function of the product or the materials it is made from. However, the visual appearance of a product can still be protected even if it serves a functional purpose.

Design registration grants the owner of the design a monopoly in that design. This means that if another person claims to have independently come up with that same design this, in itself, will not be a defence to design infringement.

This means that no-one else can copy the design without the owner's authorisation, giving them a competitive edge in the marketplace.

If a design is not registered it can be difficult to prevent another trader from adopting a similar design, especially if both products are clearly branded under different names.

In Australia designs are registered by applying to IP Australia, which is the government body that manages the design registration process. Applications can be submitted online.

Parties that can apply for design registration include:

- The designer
- An employer
- The person who commissioned the design

Similar processes operate in other countries.

Here is the catch: three important conditions must be met for a design to be registrable and enforceable against others who copy.

SECRECY

A person can only apply for design registration if a product has not been released into the marketplace, shown to the public or published (including on the internet) anywhere in the world. This means it is critical for businesses to consider, from the outset, whether their products will be one-off pieces protected by copyright law or mass-produced pieces protected by design law.

NEW AND DISTINCTIVE

The design must be new and distinctive when compared to designs that have been produced or disclosed publicly in the home market or elsewhere, or on the internet (including a business' own existing products).

Information that has been disclosed to the public in any form about a design is known as the 'prior art base'. Even if an image of the design has been published in a document anywhere in the world (as opposed to manufactured and sold), this can mean it no longer meets this requirement.

Importantly, this still applies even if the designer does not personally know about the existence of a similar design available in the global marketplace.

REGISTERED AND CERTIFIED

Last, but not least, for a design to be enforceable it must be registered and certified. In Australia, this process is administered by IP Australia. Registering and certifying your design gives you the legal right to enforce your design. This means you can take action against others using it without your permission.

HOW DO I PROTECT MY DESIGN OVERSEAS?

Generally, you will need to file protection for designs in each of your target countries.

Countries have varying definitions of terms such as 'new', as well as variations in the registration process itself. Generally, 'new' means that no identical or substantially similar design is known to have previously existed. Once a design is registered, a registration certificate is issued. Following that, the term of protection granted is generally five years, with the possibility of further renewal, in most cases for a period of up to 15 years.

- **Beware the date:** Like trademarks, the Paris Convention will allow you to claim priority to the filing date of your original design. Importantly, you need to realise if you file the same design in other countries outside this period, your design in these foreign countries may not be able to be registered as it will no longer be a new design.
- **Different strokes:** Not all countries have a separate design registration system. For example, in the USA and China to protect a design you

need to do so with a special design patent (sometimes referred to as a utility patent) which has a lower level of examination for registration than a standard patent.

CASE STUDY: Momofuku Ando

A great example of a small business using IP design rights to build a global business is the story of Mr Momofuku Ando from Japan, who invented Instant Ramen in 1958 and Cup Noodle in 1971. These days, his company, Nissin Foods, records yearly sales of 5.5 billion units in Japan alone; worldwide, nearly 100 billion portions are consumed every year, truly making the product a 'global food'.

Mr Momofuku was able to protect several aspects of his product, including the 'look' of the cup that it came in, using a patent, a trademark and a design registration. These measures prevented jealous rivals from copying his invention and eventually made him a member of international business royalty.

Protecting your innovative new process or product

The best way to protect an innovative new process or product is to apply for a patent. Broadly, patent protection is granted for a process/product that is:

- An invention
- Novel and inventive
- Useful
- Sufficiently disclosed.

In many countries, scientific theories, mathematical methods, plant or animal varieties, discoveries of natural substances, commercial methods or methods of medical treatment (as opposed to medical products) are not generally patentable.

WHAT PROTECTION DOES A PATENT GIVE?

Patent protection means an invention cannot be commercially made, used, distributed or sold without the patent owner's consent. Patent rights are usually enforced in courts that, in most systems, hold the authority to stop patent infringement. Conversely, a court can also declare a patent invalid upon a successful challenge by a third party.

WHAT RIGHTS DO PATENT OWNERS HAVE?

A patent owner has the right to decide who may – or may not – use the patented invention for the period during which it is protected. Patent owners may give permission to, or license, other parties to use their inventions on mutually agreed terms. Owners may also sell their invention rights to someone else, who then becomes the new owner of the patent. Once a patent expires, protection ends and the invention enters the public domain. This is also known as becoming 'off-patent', meaning the owner no longer holds exclusive rights to the invention, and it becomes available for commercial exploitation by others.

WHAT MAKES A PATENT VALID?

For a patent to be valid, the thing it is protecting must be new and inventive. As with designs, it is important not to disclose, demonstrate, sell or discuss an invention in public before filing a patent application. *If you must discuss the patent with others, such as investors, ensure they have a non-disclosure agreement in place before you discuss the patent with them.*

HOW DO I REGISTER A PATENT OVERSEAS?

Patents are granted by national patent offices or regional offices that carry out examination work for a group of countries. For example, the European Patent Office (EPO) and the African Intellectual Property Organisation (OAPI).

Under such regional systems, an applicant requests protection for an invention in one or more countries, and each country decides whether to offer patent protection within its borders.

Here are two ways you might go about patenting your product if you are planning to export it.

- **Option 1** – Apply directly to each of the countries/regions where you are seeking patent protection.
- **Option 2** – Use the Patent Cooperation Treaty.

The Patent Cooperation Treaty (PCT), administered by WIPO, provides for the filing of a single international patent application that has the same effect as national applications filed in the designated countries. An applicant seeking protection may file one application and request protection in as many signatory states as needed.

If you are applying from Australia, you will need to make a provisional application through IP Australia, which establishes that you are the first person to file the invention for your product in Australia. This gives you 12 months to decide whether you want to proceed with the patent.

You can then take advantage of the PCT, which:

- Lets you file a patent application in multiple countries at the same time
- Can be based on an Australian provisional application, if lodged within 12 months of the provisional application or patent filing date
- Allows you 30 months to decide if you want to pursue patent protection, and in which countries.

CASE STUDY: Stormseal

When Matthew Lennox came up with the idea for Stormseal, one of the first things he thought about was making sure his invention was patented.

A carpenter by trade, Lennox came up with the idea in 2007 when hailstones caused around half a billion dollars of insurance losses in Sydney. His product is a polyethylene film that heat shrinks to cover damaged roofs or walls, providing secure, cost-effective and lasting weather protection until permanent repairs can be made. Unlike tarpaulins they will not blow away or leak.

The first thing Lennox did was to ensure that no-one else had come up with a similar invention anywhere else in the world. Extensive internet searching convinced him that he had something new, so he thought,

"I'm going to spend my money and get a patent."

Knowing that IP protection was a vital part of his plans to commercialise Stormseal, he sought two patents – one for the chemical consistency of the Stormseal polyethylene film and another for the method of application.

As he has expanded to new markets, Lennox has expanded his patent protection. First, he sought a New Zealand patent, though has not yet opened there. Next were the UK and the US, and he has also recently applied in India and China. Stormseal can now manufacture and trade internationally with the security of patent protection.[26]

How do I protect my advertisement?

Most written works are protected under copyright, which automatically applies as soon as the work comes into existence. Copyright laws vary around the world, but there are certain treaties in place, such as the Berne Convention, that give participating countries reciprocal protection.

This effectively means that if:

- Someone based overseas copies your work, in most other countries you can still claim copyright infringement
- You reproduce a copyrighted work that was created overseas, it is likely to be an infringement as well.

Some countries have systems that allow copyright registration. For example, in the United States copyright can be registered, although registration is voluntary.

WHAT RIGHTS DO COPYRIGHT AND RELATED RIGHTS PROVIDE?

Copyright gives you the exclusive right to use or authorise others to use the work on agreed terms. The right holder(s) of a work can authorise or prohibit:

- Its reproduction in all forms, including print form and sound recording
- Its public performance and communication to the public
- Its broadcasting
- Its translation into other languages
- Its adaptation, such as from a novel to a screenplay for a film.

Similar rights of, among others, fixation (recording) and reproduction are granted under related rights.

How do I protect my software program?

There are three main forms of official protection for computer-related IP:

- Patents
- Copyright
- Circuit layout rights.

Each IP right offers a different form of protection:

- A patent protects the way the program makes a computer work.
- Copyright protects the code of a computer program from being copied.
- Circuit layout rights protect the appearance (design and layout) of an electronic circuit.

Patents offer a stronger form of protection for software.

A patent may be granted for an innovative, practical solution to a technological problem.

In summary, copyright applies as soon as the program is written. Then, depending on what it is, you may be able to protect the program with a patent.

Create an IP strategy

You have thought about what IP you have in your business and you have learned about the different types of IP rights and about how you can use them to protect your assets as you expand your business overseas.

Now, it's time to get strategic and selective about what IP you are going to protect.

IP protection is often about striking a balance between achieving maximum protection and managing IP costs. The solutions you choose to protect your IP in foreign markets will need to reflect your broader commercial business strategy.

Protecting every element of your IP in every possible potential market may seem like the safest bet, but it's probably not the most practical.

FIVE STEPS TO DEVELOP YOUR IP STRATEGY

Aside from the cost of filing registrations in multiple countries, your IP rights will also need to be asserted and maintained – and that can generate significant legal, administrative and translation costs. For example, if you are filing applications in multiple countries, all your filing costs may need to be paid upfront, potentially draining capital that you could otherwise use to develop your products and brand in your existing markets. A considered IP strategy maximises protection while minimising costs.

Step 1 – Review your international strategy

Your IP strategy will be driven by your internationalisation strategy, so it's important to be clear as early as possible what you want that to be. Ask yourself which markets offer the best potential for your product. The answer may depend on macro factors like population and national wealth – or it may come down to finding the best cultural fit.

Also consider whether you want to manage distribution yourself, or outsource to local distributors. Rather than exporting yourself, you may want to consider selling the rights to your IP to a third party to manufacture and/or distribute in specific markets.

Step 2 – Do your research

Once you have defined which countries you are interested in exporting to, look into the IP arrangements that apply in that jurisdiction.

Protecting your own IP is your first priority, but you will also need to ensure that as you expand to a new country, you do not breach someone else's IP rights.

Your product or brand may be unique in your own market, but you will need to ensure you are protected from costly legal challenges from potential competitors.

IP specialists, such as IP attorneys, can provide comprehensive searches for you, but doing your own research first can help to shape your export strategy and ensure there are no nasty surprises.

Once you file applications to protect your IP, the foreign IP offices will send you an examination report if they find deficiencies in your application. They will also let you know if your claimed IP right conflicts with those of others.

Another key aspect of researching your market is understanding how your brand will translate on foreign shores. For example, check that your product or brand's name and associated imagery translate well into other languages and cultures – and will not be considered offensive or unlucky.

In Taiwan, for example, the Taiwan Intellectual Property Office (TIPO) rejected a trademark containing the term '*taibaz*' as a trademark for bicycles, cars and spare parts. '*Taibaz*' means an upstart from Taiwan, which is used in China to disparage Taiwanese people. Use of the word as a trademark would have produced a negative impression of the Taiwanese people.

Once you have defined which countries you are interested in exporting to, investigate their IP arrangements. Search for products and brands similar to yours and check what IP protections they have in place. Check that any brand names and trademarks are appropriate for your export markets, and can be effectively translated in the native languages. The IP databases of many IP offices are freely accessible on the internet.

- UK trademark database: https://www.gov.uk/search-for-trademark
- US trademark database: https://www.uspto.gov/trademarks-application-process/search-trademark-database
- Hong Kong trademark database: https://www.ipd.gov.hk/eng/electronic_services.htm
- Vietnam trademark database: https://trademark-search.marcaria.com/en/asia/vietnam-trademark-search
- ASEAN trademark database: http://www.asean-tmview.org/tmview/welcome

Step 3 – Choose your solutions

What is the most valuable component of your IP? Is it the design of your product? Its technical features? Your brand? Or a combination of all three? Most small to medium enterprises will need to decide which element (or elements) of their product to cover with IP protection. And the answer is not always straightforward.

CASE STUDY: HEGS Pegs

When Scott Boocock first came up with the design for the HEGS peg, he protected the hook feature with a patent as this was an inventive element. But he soon realised that his IP extended much further than that.

"When we did a novelty check on the HEG peg, we discovered it had six patentable elements. We have got a patent on the hook, but also on the design, which means people cannot make a peg with bigger or smaller hooks – the whole system is protected. We have also protected the brand, and trademarked the stylised 'H'.

Boocock says that he finds the trademarks even more valuable than the patents,

"Because your brand is everything. People buy because of the brand; they buy it because of the products. They do not buy because of the patents. That is just an extra protection to prevent people from copying the HEG peg." [27]

Step 4 – Understand the costs

Protecting your IP across multiple markets can be an expensive exercise, especially if you are protecting more than one element of your product. Not long before this book went to print, I spoke to a business owner who told me that his company had applied for trademark and patent registration in multiple countries, even though most of its sales were still being made at home. He reflected (rather regretfully) that he had spent around $600,000 on IP protection. He also said that it probably would have been smarter to focus on building a successful global marketing and distribution strategy, before spending money on global IP protection.

While protecting everything upfront may be the best defence, it may prove to be financially out of reach. This is where you need to be very clear about where the value of your product lies.

If the value really is in the IP, then you need to take appropriate steps to protect it in the markets you care about most.

Balance the costs against the potential cost to your business if your product was copied and sold by a competitor with no recourse available.

HEGS Pegs founder, Boocock, agrees that if you are already selling in multiple markets, the cost of the right IP protection is well worth it. He says:

"It has cost a lot of money, over $200,000, but it does give you a lot of protection when you need it. But the money is not just lost – it's an actual asset on the balance sheet that you can sell. Every time I

go back to the valuation of the company, it's all based around that patent becoming stronger and stronger, and more valuable as the business grows."[28]

Before you start trademarking and patenting your assets, research the cost of IP protection in your target market or markets and think about how much you are prepared to invest upfront. Also consider whether there are expenses that can be deferred until later, without exposing the company to too much risk. You may find that strategies that focus on enforcement may be more cost-effective, and that you can use grace periods for filing to your advantage.

Step 5 – Get expert help

Finding the right IP strategy can be complex, and no matter how much research you do, it's likely that you will still benefit from professional IP advice. Professionals who specialise in international IP protection can offer solutions that you may have not yet considered, and can also give you access to the benefit of their experience.

CHAPTER 15

'HOW MUCH IS THIS GOING TO COST?'

CHAPTER 15

'HOW MUCH IS THIS GOING TO COST?' GETTING YOUR FUNDING AND FINANCING STRAIGHT

Before you get too far into the process of 'going global', it's crucial to get clear about the costs that you are going to incur as you expand internationally and how you are going to pay for them. This is something that business owners often ignore because it is:

- Not very exciting
- Scary to contemplate if a big investment is required upfront.

I know from experience that understanding and managing costs is one of the key challenges in 'going global', particularly for small companies. Many businesses are unaware that they will experience a significantly different set of circumstances in each market, and this is where things sometimes go wrong. There are also a bunch of costs related to global expansion that companies tend to overlook when they are still in the planning stage.

How do I know? I have made these mistakes myself, albeit on a small scale.

When I was in my twenties, I tried to start a global business from scratch, exporting artisanal goods from Morocco to Australia. I had no idea of all the different costs that I would incur and blew through $30,000 over a few months without ever making any sales. For somebody who was earning about $37,000 a year as a graduate, it was a lot of money to waste.

I know from first-hand experience that people get the financial piece wrong all the time, even when they have a lot more business experience than I had. Here are a few of the mistakes that I see them making.

- **Underestimating the cost of going global.** They put a few numbers together on the back of an envelope, and it does not look that expensive.
- **Believing they can take a cookie-cutter approach.** They assume that they will incur similar costs to what they pay at home, just in a different currency. Essentially, they make the wrong assumptions.
- **Not knowing where to get funding.** They have not informed themselves about where to get funding and suddenly they need money in a hurry.

These mistakes not only waste your time and money, they can put you under enormous financial strain and have a very negative impact on the international business. If the mistakes are serious enough, there can also be flow-on effects to the domestic business.

Knowing the numbers (even at a high level) before you need to spend the cash is key. This includes being clear on what the costs are likely to be in the new market, controlling the costs and being confident about how you are going to pay them.

You will get a much better result if you do several things:

- Map out your budgets and forecasts before you get started. It's not very exciting, but it's very important.
- Plan ahead of time how you can offset the costs of going global.
- Know where to go to get funding.

With these planks in place, you will be much better equipped to run a financially sound international operation.

Budgets and forecasts

The starting point is to create some realistic budgets and forecasts, based on research. This exercise uncovers hidden costs that might crop up during an expansion and helps you avoid nasty surprises. The kinds of costs that often surprise people include:

- Direct and indirect taxes
- Exchange rate fluctuations
- Translation costs
- Employer obligations in a foreign country
- Professional services costs

WHAT KIND OF COSTS SHOULD YOU EXPECT?

The costs that you will encounter as you go to a new country depend on the market, your mode of market entry and the size of your company. In the paragraphs below, I have listed the types of fees you will need to bear in mind, in alphabetical order.

'At the border' costs

'At the border' costs include customs duties, tariffs and, depending on what you sell, costs like fumigation and inspection.

Customs duty refers to the tax imposed on goods when they are transported across international borders. In simple terms, it is the tax that is levied on import and export of goods. Governments use this duty to raise revenues, safeguard domestic industries and regulate the movement of goods. For example, on most products imported into Australia, customs duty is 5% of the value of the goods converted to Australian dollars, but this is dependent on the type of goods.[29]

When I was trying to bring my artisanal goods into Australia back in the day, I did not know that, because they were made from natural products (leather, wood, raffia) and were packed in natural products (sawdust, wooden crates), I would have to pay hefty fees to have the goods X-rayed, fumigated and inspected. By the time I had paid those costs, I had already taken a big chunk out of my profit margin.

Banking fees

If you are going to operate in another jurisdiction, you will probably need a bank account, unless you are running a pure e-commerce business and customers are paying the money directly into a PayPal account or similar. Banking fees are generally not enormous, but they are a small expense that adds up over time.

Branding and packaging

Depending on what you are selling and where you are going, you might need to adapt your packaging or the way that you present your products – your branding. This can be true for both goods and services.

As you consider your packaging and branding, here are some questions to ask yourself:

- **Are there any regulations that I need to comply with?** Some countries – notably Middle Eastern markets – have very strict rules around packaging, information and how things are presented.

  My friend Lara Tarakjian, founder of international laser hair removal brand Silkor, recounts how she once had to take down a billboard in a Middle Eastern country. The image on the poster featured a woman smiling with her head tilted to the side, and this was considered 'too provocative' by the authorities responsible for advertising in that state.

- **What kind of packaging or presentation is going to make my company more appealing to local customers?** Brookfarm, an Australian company that produces breakfast products, had a best-selling product in Australia. It featured sleek black packaging with white writing. When Brookfarm began selling to China, they quickly discovered that black was a huge no-no for Chinese consumers (it's a colour strongly associated with death) and had to switch the packaging to feature a white packet with black writing.

Whether the changes are small tweaks or a wholesale redesign of the packaging, there will be cost to factor in.

Company registration

If you are transacting business in a country, other than through e-commerce or a distributor, you will probably need to register a company there. The cost can vary widely depending on the jurisdiction. In New Zealand, Australia or the United States, you can incorporate a company for as little as a few hundred dollars, whereas in Dubai, for example, the cost of incorporating a limited liability company is close to USD 7,000, not including bank account opening fees and professional costs.

Foreign exchange

Small companies going global for the first time are often unaware of the costs of foreign exchange. But currency market volatility can quickly turn a profit overseas into a loss.

- Step one here is to understand what your exposure is, and any business that operates with an international currency in play is at risk. If your local currency drops relative to the market where you are selling, your input prices increase. Similarly, if your local currency rises, it can damage your competitiveness in foreign markets, because your products become more expensive for your customers, or your profit margin takes a hit.
- Step two is to prepare a foreign exchange management policy and set out parameters detailing how much foreign exchange risk you are prepared to accept and for how long.
- Step three is to get a handle on what tools you already use to mitigate foreign exchange risk and what tools you might need going forward.

Most businesses (even larger ones) do not turn their attention to foreign exchange until a negative fluctuation hits their profit margin. I highly recommend speaking to a trustworthy foreign exchange provider before you get deep into your international business. That way you can get insights on how to limit exchange rate risk and your options for doing so – before you receive a nasty surprise at the hands of global markets.

Freight costs

If you are shipping goods, you will need to account for the cost of freight, including the cost of preparing your export documentation. Freight costs rose astronomically during COVID-19 and, in 2021, were 25% higher than at the start of 2020.

Government service fees

In some countries, companies must pay a range of fees – in addition to the company registration fee – to operate a business in the jurisdiction. For example, if you are setting up in the United Arab Emirates, you will need to pay a municipality waste fee, a Ministry of Economy fee, a Chamber of Commerce fee – because being a member of the Chamber of Commerce is compulsory – and a 'commercial services improvement fee', which goes towards improving the quality of service in government departments. Off the top of your head, you would never guess that any of those fees applied. As you go to register and set-up overseas, it's worth digging down and seeing what additional government charges you are going to be up for.

Intellectual property registration fees

As we discussed in Chapter 14, you will need to register your intellectual property (IP) to ensure it is not ripped off in a foreign market. IP theft is a real problem for businesses and the more markets you go into, the higher the risk of having your IP stolen.

That is why you need to cover your back and make sure that your IP is registered in each country that you go to. Although this is an expensive exercise, it's a means of preventing commercial disputes and can save you a lot of money (and heartache) down the track.

Licensing

In some countries, you need a licence to operate a company in particular industries. A licensing fee is an amount of money that you pay the government for the privilege of performing a service or engaging in a certain line of work.

If there is a mutual recognition of qualifications between your home market and the new market, you may be able to use the licence that you have at home, and simply pay to have it translated into the language of the country that you are operating in.

Marketing

Marketing to a new country is an involved process and it's likely that you will need to develop a new marketing strategy and materials and campaigns that are different to those you have used at home.

Marketing expenses can range from the traditional ones – trade show fees, booths, banners, brochures, schwag – right through to reproducing your website in another language and associated translation and localisation costs, search engine optimisation and social media campaigns. None of this stuff is free.

Marketing costs can mount up very quickly and this can be dangerous if you are in the early stages of figuring out which marketing will work – there is no point pouring a big chunk of your cash away on marketing if it's not generating you a commensurate return.

TIP Track what you spend on marketing and what volume of sales you generate from it, month by month.

Notary fees

A notary is a person with legal training who is authorised to perform certain legal formalities such as drawing up or certifying contracts, deeds and other documents for use in other jurisdictions.

When it comes to international expansion, a notary certifies that your documents are what they purport to be. In many countries, most of your documentation, including immigration paperwork, identity documents and company registrations from your home jurisdiction, will need to be notarised in order to be official in the eyes of the government. Notary fees are not enormous, although it depends to some extent on how many pieces of documentation you need notarised. It might be a few hundred dollars or a few thousand, but it's worth keeping an eye on as all the little bits and pieces add up over time.

Professional fees

As you start selling or setting up overseas, there are a range of professional fees that you might encounter.

If you need to draft heads of agreement or contracts, or you want to incorporate a company overseas, there will be legal fees to pay.

If you have entities set-up in other jurisdictions and want to funnel money back to the home country, you will need tax advice and a competent accountant who understands international business and can assist you with the accounting and reporting requirements for foreign jurisdictions.

You may also require the support of strategy or market entry consultants, or other kinds of specialised help as you set-up overseas.

Rent and overheads

If you are setting up a presence in-country and you are not fortunate enough to have a strategic alliance partner who can loan you office space, you will need to think about how you will set-up your office and what it will cost.

- Will you rent or buy?
- Will you use a serviced office?
- Will you have an office in a central location or somewhere out of the centre, which will be less expensive?
- What is the median price of office space in the city that you are expanding into? (This will give you a ballpark of how much you might expect to pay on things like rent.)

Each of these factors can have an impact on how much you end up paying. When you are choosing your office set-up overseas, make sure that you tailor it to what your business can realistically bear.

I have a friend who came out of the corporate world – a large investment banking firm – and set-up a business with colleagues in London. They sourced $1 million worth of investment to start up and hired the flashiest office that they could find in Mayfair. When I asked if he needed such an expensive office and if he would be able to pay for it, my friend said,

"Don't worry. We have a million dollars of investment."

Six months later, the group was still struggling to get more than a trickle of clients and the expensive office in Mayfair was draining their bank account dry.

The moral of the story: as you set-up overseas, consider what the costs you incur abroad will mean for your business as a whole.

Sponsor fees

A sponsor fee is payable in some countries where you are sponsoring an employee to come from another country and work in a third market. If you are building an office tower in Saudi Arabia and you bring in a Pakistani workforce, you will have to sponsor them and pay for your team to be in-country. Fees vary from place to place, but can be significant.

Travel expenses

As you are planning your budget, think about how much you will need to spend on travel and what it is likely to cost to do the travel required to get your international business up and running.

In the pre-COVID world, I knew one business owner who was flying between Sydney, Australia and Dublin, Ireland every six weeks. Although that kind of travel is off the table for the foreseeable future, the reality is that you will need to include some travel in your international expansion plans.

Consider the next 12 and 24 months – how many times will you fly into your target market? How many of your team will travel? Will you fly business class, or can you handle being on an economy flight for 20 hours and still be functional the day you arrive? Do you have frequent flyer points that you can use?

Think about where you will stay while you are in-market. Will you book a five-star hotel, rent an AirBnB or crash on a friend's couch? Will you pay $350 a night plus $100 a day for food and incidentals, or raid your friend's fridge and take her a $50 bottle of wine as a thank you?

Do not forget about how you will get around while you are in-market either. Will you jump on a fast train from the airport to the city centre or do you expect to be collected in a limousine? Are you getting a rickshaw between meetings, or walking? Are you going to be up for a couple of hundred dollars in transport costs for each visit, or a couple of thousand? Individually, ground transport costs are relatively low, but they can really mount up over a year. I am embarrassed to say that I am closely acquainted with someone who once spent $7,000 on taxis in 12 months.

Each of these travel decisions affects your international budget, and are worth spending a little time on.

Visas

Depending on where you are from and where you are operating internationally, you may only have to bear minimal costs associated with immigration and visas. However, if you or employees from your home office plan to work in the target country, you will need to get a business or resident's visa.

Sometimes, even tourist visas can be expensive. I recall a particularly memorable trip to Saudi Arabia a few years ago, when I travelled to the Middle East with my six-month old son and his grandmother. I ended up leaving them in Dubai and going to Riyadh alone, as it seemed unreasonable to pay $1,500 per person for tourist visas for a two-day visit.

Offsetting the costs

Once you have put together your forecasts and budgets, think about how to go about offsetting the costs that you are going to incur as you go global.

Reflecting on the following questions is a good starting point.

- Will you need to adjust your prices to absorb these expenses?
- Can you take advantage of free trade agreements to reduce your cost to customers?
- How could you control your production costs to drive better margins?
- Will you be able to sell enough units of your product or service to enough clients in the new market to offset the overheads and the cost of goods sold?
- How else could you offset the costs that are coming up?
- Will the return on investment in the new market be attractive enough?

Once you have an understanding of the cost base, do the exercise of working out what you want the profit to be and then work out how much you need to sell and at what price point to make that a reality.

How will we pay for this?

Once you have worked out how much going global is going to cost and how to mitigate that expense, it's time to work out how to pay for it.

This is a topic that deserves its own book, but I will cover the various avenues here in very general terms.

BANKS

Banks are a traditional port of call for companies looking for funding for an international expansion. As well as garden variety products like overdrafts and lines of credit, banks also provide financial products specifically targeted to international trade.

For example, if your international operating cycle (the length of time it takes to sell your inventory overseas and collect the money) exceeds the credit terms extended by your suppliers, you will have a financing requirement. A bank will be able to provide export finance to cover the gap between when you can turn inventory and trade receivables to cash and when you must pay suppliers.

Banks also provide Letters of Credit, Documentary Collection, bank guarantees and trade credit insurance.

Of course, banks make money from loaning money and facilitating transactions, so their services are not free of charge!

BOOTSTRAPPING

If you are extremely clever, or very lucky, you may be able to bootstrap your international expansion – build it from the ground up using only personal savings and cash flow from your existing business.

Bootstrapping only works if you have either very low setup costs or lots of spare cash, otherwise it is a soul-crushingly slow way to build an international business. However, its unfair advantage is that it enables you to keep 100% of your company's equity and avoid ceding control to external parties.

INVESTORS

If you need extra cash to get your international business going, you may consider getting an investor – private equity, venture capital or angel – to provide the funds.

The upside of investors is that you do not need to repay the investment on the same terms and at the same speed as you would repay a bank. The downside is that you cede partial control of your business to the investor, whenever he or she takes an equity stake (and if you do too many rounds of investment, you may end up owning only a small stake in your company).

CROWDFUNDING

If traditional investors are not your cup of tea, you may like to consider crowdfunding to source additional funds for your international expansion Crowdfunding uses small amounts of capital from a large number of individuals to finance a new business venture. It relies heavily on accessing vast networks of people through crowdfunding websites and social media to bring investors and entrepreneurs together. The genius of crowdfunding is its potential to increase entrepreneurship by expanding the pool of investors beyond the traditional circle of owners, relatives and venture capitalists.

GOVERNMENT LOANS AND GRANTS

Governments in many countries have schemes to support both exporters and, in some cases, companies investing into their jurisdiction.

Australia

In Australia, the Federal Government's Export Market Development Grant enables companies exporting internationally to claim up to 50% of moneys spent promoting their business in international markets.

Export Finance Australia, the Federal government's export credit agency, supports SMEs and corporates to sell in international markets by providing financial expertise and solutions including loans, guarantees, bonds and insurance options.

AusIndustry – the Federal Government agency for delivering services to support industry, research and innovation – has a range of grants available for different industry sectors, many of them relevant to businesses 'going global'.

Australia's State and Territory governments also offer a range of grants and loans for various industry sectors, which are worth investigating as you investigate international expansion.

Singapore

Enterprise Singapore, Singapore's national enterprise development agency, assists Singaporean businesses with financing. Its offering includes the Capability Development Grant, which is aimed at providing SMEs with financial assistance to defray up to 70% of costs, relating to consultancy, human resources development, productivity development and business capability development, amongst others.

USA

The United States offers a wide range of financial support to companies operating internationally through its Export-Import Bank (EXIM) and a suite of other financial products provided by the US Department of Agriculture (USDA), the Department of Commerce (DOC) and the Small Business Administration (SBA).

The SBA, for example, has three loan programs for international trade – the Export Express program, the Export Working Capital Loan and the International Trade Loan, and the USDA offers an Export Credit Guarantee and a Facility Guarantee Program to companies operating in the agricultural sector.

The examples above are a small sample of the mechanisms that governments around the world use to provide financial support for companies going global. As you put together your plan for international expansion, do not forget to investigate what sort of support the government in your country can offer.

CHAPTER 16

BUILDING A GLOBAL TEAM

CHAPTER 16

BUILDING A GLOBAL TEAM

And, finally, building a global team.

Choosing who is in your international team is just as important as choosing the right market or the right distributor, or any of the other topics that we have covered in the last fifteen chapters. The team is the vehicle that will deliver your global vision for you – these are the folks who are going to get stuff done.

As this book goes to print, we are in the throes of a global pandemic. How we work, both at home and abroad, has changed dramatically as a result. But, I'll let you into a secret. The first draft of this chapter was begun several years ago, before anyone (apart from the experts) had even considered a pandemic. At Dearin & Associates, we were already building a global team and working successfully across national borders. We were a global virtual team. These days, the team functions seamlessly between the East, West and South coasts of Australia; San Francisco and Chicago, USA; the Philippines; and India. We also have satellite teams in Dubai, Egypt, Singapore, Vietnam and the UK.

While most of the world has taken up working remotely as a crisis measure, we have seen it as the future for several years, and one of the most sensible ways of working for smaller companies starting out in the international space. It is a model that is flexible, agile and relatively inexpensive.

In this chapter, I want to show you how you can use the same structure. I will suggest a couple of other options as well.

Before COVID-19, there was a lot of scepticism about whether virtual teams could actually work because, for the majority of people, they did not. While I believe that, overall, people's ability to work remotely has improved since the pandemic began and other options were removed, it is still not an area that is well understood. Most companies have no process for creating a virtual team, and no tools or strategy for managing one – if they get as far as setting it up. The result can be a lot of team dysfunction because the wrong people are running in all directions without knowing where they are heading, why they are heading there, or how they will get there. Here are some of the symptoms:

- No-one is really clear about what they are supposed to be doing
- Nobody is across what anyone else is doing
- People are not clear on the 'big vision'
- Work is over budget and behind schedule
- The team feels demotivated

The secret to global teamwork is having the right team, with the right tools and managing them the right way. Global team building is a huge topic. In this chapter, I will just focus on the initial steps to create a strong global team.

Choose the right process to create your global team

Thinking internationally when it comes to team recruitment does not just increase the size of your talent pool. It makes you more fit to tackle global markets, because you work with people who understand the customers in the countries you are in. For example, if you are selling to Japan, having someone on your team who speaks Japanese and understands Japan's commercial environment is a huge plus.

WHO DO WE NEED ON THE TEAM?

The first step to creating your global team is to work out who you need. I suggest you review your strategic plan and your three-, two- and one-year goals for international expansion. Use those as a guide to who you should be hiring, where and when.

OPTIONS FOR CREATING A GLOBAL TEAM

You have several options when it comes to creating a global team. You can:

- Send some of your existing staff to the new market
- Build a new team in the new market
- Hire contractors in the new market
- Use team members in third countries (especially for back-office roles such as virtual assistants, designers and accountants).

Send staff overseas

Sending one of your existing team members overseas can be an effective strategy, if you have the right person making the move for the right reasons. There are a couple of arguments in favour of this approach: the person or people who are moving overseas already know the company and their role in it. They understand the company culture, know what needs to be done, and have already earned a high level of trust.

On the downside, taking a team member from the home team and sending them to a new country can disrupt the domestic operation and be personally disruptive for the team member. He or she may not know the new country, how it works, or how to do business there, all of which can be stressful. It is also expensive to relocate a team member to a new country.

This approach only works if you have a highly competent and trustworthy team member who is willing and able to take on the challenge of moving overseas and personally resilient enough to deal with the challenges that will inevitably crop up.

Establish your team in-country

If you do not have people on your team who are willing to relocate to a new country, you might also choose to establish a completely new team in your target market. The upsides of this option are that local hires know the culture of the target market and how things work. You get immediate ears and eyes on the ground, and insights into what you need to do to succeed in the new place. Depending on where you are operating, building a team in-country may also be much less expensive and disruptive than relocating a team member from headquarters.

One of my clients is an Australian manufacturing firm which sells products to 35 countries, primarily via distributors. It also has an office in Chicago, Illinois, which is its North American headquarters. Pre-COVID, the founder and his wife relocated to the United States on a semi-permanent basis and split their time between Australia and the US for three or four years. During that time, they built and managed a team on the ground, which continued to run when they returned to Australia.

It is not all upside though. For starters, you will have a lower initial level of trust with a new hire, working outside the company headquarters. It will take time to build this trust and for the new hire to adjust to the culture of your company. This can sometimes be quite a process, as you juggle both international and corporate cultural differences.

Building a team in-country can also be expensive if your team needs a physical office to work from, and there can be complexity in dealing with local labour laws and regulations.

If you want to build a team in-country without having to set up the management and back-office infrastructure, you may want to consider using an Employer of Record (EOR) arrangement. An Employer of Record is a company or organisation that is legally responsible for paying employees, including dealing with employee taxes, benefits, insurance, visa application, sponsorship applications and other human resources functions. You manage the performance of your employee, but the EOR takes care of everything else, including the employee's payroll.

Hire contractors in-country

If you like the idea of a team on the ground in your target market, but do not want the risk of full-time staff, you may prefer to hire contractors on the ground.

The advantage of the contractor model is that it is often less expensive and disruptive than relocating a team member from HQ. The approach may also be more flexible, as you can hire and fire more easily, or hire for fixed periods of time, depending on your requirements.

However, there are downsides to working with contractors in-market. You will almost certainly experience a lower initial level of trust between your company and a new contractor, working outside your headquarters.

Not only do you not know each other, the new contractor is also unfamiliar with your company culture. In addition, because contractors often do not work for your company full-time, they can be less 'tethered' to the company than permanent staff. This sometimes makes them harder to monitor and more of a flight risk, especially if they find a full-time opportunity elsewhere. None of these factors are insurmountable hurdles, but it does take time to build trust and a solid working relationship.

Hire distributors in-country

Depending on what you sell, you may prefer to create your first 'global team' by setting up distribution agreements for your new territory.

Working with distributors is similar to working with contractors, insofar as it relieves you of HR risk. Remember, however, that even if you sign on with a distributor, you cannot just walk away and leave them to get on with it. Managing distributors is a little like managing staff: you need to motivate and inspire them and measure their performance on an ongoing basis. It is a relationship that requires an active approach if you want to get the best from a distributor team. And, in many markets, distribution agreements are hard to terminate, so if things go sour, you may be left with a sticky situation on your hands.

Create a Global Virtual Team

At the other end of the spectrum, you can source your team from around the world and run a global virtual team (GVT) – 100% remote and virtual.

The upside of this approach is that it's cost effective, you get access to great talent, and you can service multiple time zones.

One of my clients is an Australian affiliate marketing company expanding to South East Asia. The company is headquartered in Sydney. Before it began its global play, the CEO set up a team in Malaysia, to service the Australian market. The Malaysia office became the regional headquarters for the South East Asian expansion and is staffed by a Malay team. The company has also begun hiring developers in other locations in Asia, to keep up with its product development demands.

Often GVTs involve more complexity than monocultural teams located in one place. This is because they are diverse and there are greater cultural differences between team members. Decision-making may also be more complex and all these factors make them harder to manage. GVTs require robust systems and a highly structured team culture to work well.

Your first task is to work out which kind of global team is most suitable for you, now and in the future.

Hiring a global team

As you start to think about where to recruit your global team, it's important to realise that supply may exist in 'hubs' that hold remarkable potential for geo-targeted global recruiting. In other words, if you know where to look, there may be lots of suitable candidates who would fit the role you are trying to fill, and who may be willing to do so on a competitive basis. For example, in 2021, Vietnam is the place to source a full-stack developer, the Philippines is great for operations roles and designers, and you cannot go past India for accountants.

Depending on the role, you might look to recruit in your new target market, from your home market or a third market.

As you survey the world for talent, be aware that regional priorities and perceptions of total compensation and non-financial compensation can vary significantly. Despite the rapid globalisation that the world has experienced over the last decade, candidates' perceptions of what they are looking for in a role are shaped by regional culture and other factors.

For example, in the Asia-Pacific region, people generally expect to work in only a few jobs or for long periods throughout their careers. In Europe, workers are sceptical that companies will allow them to define their own work schedules. What you offer candidates needs to line up with regional expectations: APAC talent's intent is to be loyal to an employer and European talent's desire is to have flexible workplace arrangements. If you understand the trends in regional perception and priorities, you will be more successful at attracting the right staff to grow your company overseas.

WHAT KIND OF PEOPLE ARE WE LOOKING FOR?

When it comes down to it there are three questions you need to answer when it comes to any potential new recruit, at home or offshore.

- Can they do the work?
- Will they do the work?
- Will they 'fit' with the rest of the team?

That being said, exactly what sort of people do you want in your global team? I believe that, as you build a global team, you should ideally be looking for people who have a deep understanding of your industry and a deep knowledge of the markets you want to operate in. If it is relevant to the role, they should be willing to travel, make cold calls to other companies as needed and work odd hours to accommodate different time zones.

Your ideal candidates will also share your drive and mission to make your company global. This is even more important when your team is dispersed rather than centralised, because you have fewer means of motivating them. They need to be able to get excited without you pushing them on a daily basis.

If you are hiring for a GVT, you will need people who are autonomous by nature and comfortable working without explicit instructions and fixed schedules. To be a virtual worker requires the ability to work independently and to take initiative, because you are not surrounded by team members who will prompt you to act. A person who is not self-directed may have a hard time fitting into a GVT. They will constantly feel that the manager is not giving enough instructions and will feel lost because the work environment lacks structure.

Your remote team members should also be good communicators. A lot of your interaction is likely to be through written communication, so make sure the person can write to-the-point messages that are easy to understand. Communication is the only tool in the manager's toolbox for improving the team and achieving goals.

These skills and traits can be taught and are acquired with experience, but I recommend that you check them off before hiring a new person – otherwise, the team, the employee and the manager will struggle during the adaptation process.

APPENDICES

ENDNOTES & REFERENCES

ENDNOTES

1 Elaborately Transformed Manufactures (ETM) are generally what would be termed 'finished goods'. ETM covers a vast range of goods, including machinery, whitegoods and other household wares, motor vehicles, clothing and footwear and can be distinguished from Simply Transformed Manufactures and Processed Primary Products. *In Focus 2017 – Australian Made*, [https://bluenotes.anz.com/content/dam/bluenotes/documents/ANZ_Manufacturing_AustralianMade.pdf], p7.

2 *Domestic electronics market in India to reach $400 bn by 2025*, Invest India, [https://www.investindia.gov.in/sector/electronic-systems#:~:text=Industry%20Scenario,-Domestic%20electronics%20market&text=The%20electronics%20market%20valued%20at,and%20other%20industrial%20electronic%20products] Accessed 31 March 2021.

3 Global IOT Market Analysis, [https://www.prnewswire.com/in/news-releases/global-internet-of-things-iot-market-size-was-valued-at-usd-164-billion-in-2018-and-is-expected-to-grow-at-a-cagr-of-38-62-by-2025-valuates-reports-842976853.html], 21 January 2020.

4 A 2013 study by the Melbourne Institute of Applied Economic and Social Research found that 'learning by exporting' was a driver of innovation among small and medium enterprises (SMEs).

5 *The $150m Aussie brand that Australia rejected: Sean Ashby, aussieBum*, mybusiness, 28 July 2017. [https://www.mybusiness.com.au/marketing/3166-sean-ashby-aussiebum] Accessed 31 March 2021..

6 'Qatar crisis: Businesses caught in crossfire as dispute hits companies', *Express*, 30 June 2017, [https://www.express.co.uk/news/world/823180/qatar-crisis-boycott-dispute-business-companies-hit]. Accessed 27 April 2018.

7 Dealing with political instability in foreign markets, *Powerlinx*, by Hassan Spruill, 6 July, 2016, [https://www.powerlinx.com/blog/dealing-with-political-instability-in-foreign-markets/], Accessed 26 April, 2018.

8 'What's at stake in the looming US-China trade war: the full list', *The Financial Times*, Joanna S Kao, Ed Crooks and Jane Pong April 18, 2018, [https://ig.ft.com/us-china-tariffs/] Accessed 25 April, 2018.

9 'U.S.-China Trade War Is Bad News for Google's Expansion', *Wall Street Journal*, Douglas MacMillan and Liza Lin, April 22, 2018, [https://www.wsj.com/articles/googles-android-expansion-mired-in-u-s-china-trade-war-1524398404]. Accessed 25 April, 2018.

10 Della Rosa wins a major slice of Chinese business, Austrade, October 2017, [https://www.austrade.gov.au/australian/export/free-trade-agreements/fta-case-studies/della-rosa-wins-a-major-slice-of-chinese-business] Accessed 31 March 2021.

11 *Daigou* literally translated means 'buying on behalf of'. It refers to a network of shopping agents who buy things for residents on mainland China that are unavailable or hard to find there. Essentially, it is a channel of commerce between mainland Chinese buyers and overseas professional shoppers, sometimes referred to as the 'grey market'.

12 *Why Starbucks Failed in Australia*, CNBC, 26 July 2018 [https://youtu.be/_FGUkxn5kZQ

13 *Gillette's Latest Innovation in Razors: the 11-Cent Blade*, Wall Street Journal, 1 October 2010, [https://www.wsj.com/articles/SB10001424052748704789404575524273890970954]

14 This is changing to some degree because of the vast amount of business that is transacted with the West.

15 Ramos, D. C. (2014). High context. In S. Thompson (Ed.), *Encyclopedia of diversity and social justice*. Lanham, MD: Rowman & Littlefield Publishers. Retrieved from [http://db19.linccweb.org/login?url=https://search.credoreference.com/content/entry/rowmandasj/high_context/0?institutionId=6086]

16 'Scale Up Your Business with Vanessa Garrard, Founder of SourceHub', Episode 30, *Business Beyond Borders Podcast*, [https://dearinassociates.com/podcast/episode-30-vanessa-garrard-founder-of-sourcehub-group/]

17 'E-Commerce in China: A Guide for Australian Business', Austrade, February 2016.

18 *Franchising Your Business: Advantages and Disadvantages*, InternicolaLaw Firm, [https://www.franchiselawsolutions.com/franchising/franchising-advantages-disadvantages/]

19 [https://www.linklaters.com/en/insights/publications/2018/july/cross-border-joint-ventures]. Accessed 18 January 2021.

20 [https://www.dwt.com/-/media/files/publications/2012/05/international-joint-ventures-a-practical-approach/files/international-joint-ventures-article_stewart/fileattachment/international-joint-ventures-article_stewart.pdf] Accessed 18 January 2021.

21 [https://www.globaltrademag.com/pros-cons-international-joint-ventures/]. Accessed 18 January 2021

22 [https://dealroom.net/blog/benefits-of-mergers-and-acquisitions]. Accessed 19 January 2021.

23 [https://www.thedrum.com/industryinsights/2019/01/11/seven-big-benefits-international-mergers-acquisitions]. Accessed 19 January 2021.

24 [https://www.firstanguilla.com/8-legal-tax-benefits-of-owning-an-offshore-business/] Accessed 19 January 2021.

25 [https://www.expatica.com/working/self-employment/offshore-companies-18156/#disadvantages] Accessed 19 January 2021.

26 *Case Study: Success Story – Patent protection as a business grows*, IP Australia, [https://www.ipaustralia.gov.au/patents/engaging-an-attorney-toolkit/case-study-success-story] Accessed 6 April 2021.

27 *Protecting Your Intellectual Property Overseas*, Export Finance and Investment Corporation, 2017 [https://www.exportfinance.gov.au/media/4889/efic-protecting-your-ip-overseas-specialist-paper.pdf] Accessed 19 May 2017. p10

28 Ibid

29 *GST, Customs Duty & Importing Business Goods to Australia FAQ [2019 Update]*, International Accounting Solutions, [https://intas.com.au/importing-business-goods-australia/#:~:text=On%20most%20products%20imported%20into,correct%20amount%20of%20customs%20duty] Accessed 26 March 2021

REFERENCES

Chapter 4

- 'Political stability and instability', [http://textbook.stpauls.br/business_organization/page_62.htm] Accessed 25 April 2018.
- 'Changes in Political Stability Impact Business Markets in Emerging Markets', *Euromonitor International*, [https://blog.euromonitor.com/2014/11/changes-in-political-stability-impact-business-environments-in-emerging-markets.html] Accessed 25 April 2018.
- 'What is at stake in the looming US-China trade war: the full list', *The Financial Times*, Joanna S Kao, Ed Crooks and Jane Pong April 18, 2018, [https://ig.ft.com/us-china-tariffs/] Accessed 25 April, 2018.
- 'Free Trade Agreements: What is an FTA and what are the benefits?', ABC News, by Matthew Grimson, 8 April 2014 [http://www.abc.net.au/news/2014-04-07/free-trade-agreement-explained-bilateral-fta-tpp/5371314]
- 'The Basics of Tariffs And Trade Barriers', *Investopedia*, Brent Radcliffe, 4 April, 2018 [https://www.investopedia.com/articles/economics/08/tariff-trade-barrier-basics.asp] Accessed 26 April 2018.
- *Tariff and Non-tariff Barriers to Trade*, Dan Sumner, Vince Smith, and Parr Rosson, [https://www.iatp.org/files/Tariff_and_Non-tariff_Barriers_to_Trade.htm] Accessed 26 April 2018.
- 'Non-tariff barriers', *Institute for Government*, [https://www.instituteforgovernment.org.uk/explainers/non-tariff-barriers] Accessed 26 April 2018.
- 'Non-tariff barriers and how they impact your business', *The Manzella Report*, John Manzella, 1 July 2001, [http://www.manzellareport.com/index.php/trade-finance/366-tariffs-and-non-tariff-barriers-and-how-they-impact-your-business] Accessed 26 April 2018.
- 'How Time Zones Affect Global Businesses', *Entrepreneur*, Mark Henricks, 1 June 2006, [https://www.entrepreneur.com/article/160228] Accessed 26 April 2018.
- [http://reports.weforum.org/global-enabling-trade-2013/3-description-of-supply-chain-barriers-to-trade/] Accessed 27 April 2018.
- *Doing Business: Measuring Business Regulations*, Simeon Djankov, 2017 [http://www.doingbusiness.org/data] Accessed 27 April 2018.
- *Protecting Your Intellectual Property Overseas – What you can do to keep control of your IP in the global marketplace*, EFIC, IP Australia, February 2017. [https://www.efic.gov.au/media/3680/efic-protecting-your-ip-overseas-specialist-paper.pdf] Accessed 27 April 2018.

- '3% of Americans Still Use Dial-Up Internet', *Fast Company*, 26 August, 2013, [https://www.fastcompany.com/3016298/3-of-americans-still-use-dial-up-internet] Accessed 27 April, 2018.
- 'What is Daigou?', *Sydney Morning Herald*, Lucy Battersby, 14 June 2016, [https://www.smh.com.au/business/companies/what-is-daigou-20160614-gpixf4.html] Accessed 27 April 2018.
- 'Australia's internet speeds lag behind world, despite NBN', *Sydney Morning Herald*, Chris Jager, 15 March 2017, [https://www.smh.com.au/technology/australias-internet-speeds-lag-behind-world-20170315-guyh4u.html] Accessed 27 April 2018.
- 'Qatar crisis: what you need to know', *BBC News*, 19 July 2017, [http://www.bbc.com/news/world-middle-east-40173757] Accessed 27 April 2018.
- 'Qatar crisis: Businesses caught in crossfire as dispute hits companies', *Express*, 30 June 2017, [https://www.express.co.uk/news/world/823180/qatar-crisis-boycott-dispute-business-companies-hit] Accessed 27 April 2018.
- 'Kazakhstan, Ukraine and Guam are among the 54 countries that have faster fixed broadband than Australia', *SBS News*, Nick Baker, 8 January 2018, [https://www.sbs.com.au/news/kazakhstan-ukraine-found-to-have-faster-broadband-than-australia] Accessed 27 April 2018.

Chapter 5

- *What are Firmographics?* [http://www.wiglafjournal.com/marketing/2013/01/what-are-firmographics/] Accessed 21 May 2021.
- *Four Types of Market Segmentation with Examples.* [https://blog.alexa.com/types-of-market-segmentation/]
- *Value Proposition Design*, Alex Osterwalder & Yves Pigneur, 10 October 2014.

Chapter 6

- *Monetizing Innovation*, Madhavan Ramanujam and Georg Tacke, 2016, John Wiley & Sons Inc, Hoboken, New Jersey.
- *Gillette's Latest Innovation in Razors: the 11-Cent Blade*, Wall Street Journal, 1 October 2010, [https://www.wsj.com/articles/SB10001424052748704789404575524273890970954]

Chapter 8

- [https://www.betterhelp.com/advice/stereotypes/what-are-some-common-stereotypes-and-why/] Accessed 7 April 2021.
- [https://www.simplypsychology.org/katz-braly.html] accessed 7 April 2021.

- [https://www.shippingsolutions.com/blog/knowing-your-place-in-international-business] accessed 7 April 2021.
- *Understanding International Business Culture: Using Collectivism to Your Advantage*, Becky Destigter, International Trade Blog, 8 September 2013.
- [https://www.shippingsolutions.com/blog/understanding-international-business-culture-using-collectivism-to-your-advantage] accessed 8 April 2021.
- *How Different Cultures Understand Time*, Richard Lewis, Insider, 2 June 2014, [https://www.businessinsider.com/how-different-cultures-understand-time-2014-5?IR=T] accessed 8 April 2021.
- *The Culture Map: Breaking Through the Invisible Boundaries of Global Business*, Erin Meyer, 6 December 2014.
- *Camels, sheikhs and Billionaires: your guide to business culture in the Middle East and North Africa*, Cynthia Dearin, 2015.
- *Cultural Differences in Business Communication*, John Hooker, December 2008, Tepper School of Business, Carnegie Mellon University. [https://public.tepper.cmu.edu/jnh/businessCommunication.pdf]

Chapter 9

- 'E-Commerce', *Investopedia*, [https://www.investopedia.com/terms/e/ecommerce.asp] Accessed 20 June, 2018.
- 'E-Commerce in China: A Guide for Australian Business', Austrade, February 2016.
- *Franchising Your Business: Advantages and Disadvantages*, InternicolaLaw Firm, [https://www.franchiselawsolutions.com/franchising/franchising-advantages-disadvantages/]
- *A Global Strategic Guide to International Franchising*, the balance small business, 26 November 2018, [https://www.thebalancesmb.com/international-franchising-a-global-strategic-initiative-1953329]
- *Technology Licensing Guidebook*, [https://www.umass.edu/tto/sites/default/files/Technology%20Licensing%20Guidebook.pdf]
- *Using foreign direct investment as an international market entry strategy*, TradeReady, 21 November 2014, [http://www.tradeready.ca/2014/fittskills-refresher/foreign-direct-investment-international-market-entry-strategy/http://www.tradeready.ca/2014/fittskills-refresher/foreign-direct-investment-international-market-entry-strategy/]
- *Top 10 Strategic Alliance Examples For You to Gain Insight From*, ReferralRock, [https://referralrock.com/blog/strategic-alliance-examples/]
- *Strategic Alliances: Three Ways To Make Them Work*, Steve Steinhilber, Harvard Business Press, 2008.

Chapter 10

- *Freight and logistics*, Guide to Exporting, Austrade, [https://www.austrade.gov.au/Australian/Export/Guide-to-exporting/Freight-and-logistics]
- *International Logistics*, Export.gov, [https://2016.export.gov/logistics/index.asp]
- 'HS Codes: A Beginner's Guide for Imports and Exports', International Cargo Express [https://www.icecargo.com.au/hs-codes-beginners-guide/] accessed 11 March 2021.
- *How to Export from Australia, The Easy 7-Step Guide*, International Cargo Express, [https://www.icecargo.com.au/export-from-australia/] accessed 12 March 2021.
- *How to Fill in an Airway Bill*, Fedex, [https://shippingchannel.fedex.com/en-gb/customs-clearance/air-waybill.html] accessed 12 March 2021.
- *Shipping Air or Ocean Freight*, Freightos, [https://www.freightos.com/freight-resources/air-freight-vs-ocean-freight-making-the-decision/#:~:text=Air%20freight%20is%20faster%2C%20safer,comes%20to%20shipping%20hazardous%20materials] Accessed 15 March 2021.
- [https://www.icecargo.com.au/shipping-documentation-guide/#:~:text=Packing%20List,goods%20are%20directed%20for%20inspection] Accessed 15 March 2021.

Chapter 11

- *Getting paid*, Export Finance Australia, [https://www.exportfinance.gov.au/resources-news/exporter-journey/getting-paid/] accessed 15 March 2021.
- *Methods of Payment*, International Trade Administration, [https://www.trade.gov/methods-payment] accessed 16 March 2021.
- *Overseas Customers – getting paid*, Law Donut, [https://www.lawdonut.co.uk/business/contracts-disputes/debt-recovery/overseas-customers-getting-paid] accessed 16 March 2021.
- *Letters of Credit*, [https://www.nibusinessinfo.co.uk/content/advantages-and-disadvantages-letters-credit] accessed 16 March 2021.
- *The pros and cons of different payment terms*, EDC, [https://www.edc.ca/en/article/different-payment-terms.html] accessed 16 March 2021.

Chapter 12

- *Three Main Differences between the US and China in Consumer Marketing*, Jin Zhang, LinkedIn, 7 April 2015, [https://www.linkedin.com/pulse/three-main-differences-between-us-china-consumer-marketing-jin-zhang/] Accessed 17 March 2021.
- *Raft of food safety scandals has shaken Chinese consumers*, N Business, 9 July 2013, [https://www.thenationalnews.com/business/raft-of-food-safety-scandals-has-shaken-chinese-consumers-1.589647] accessed 17 March 2021.
- *Marketing in China: How Chinese audiences differ from Western audiences*, MarketMeChina, 14 January 2020. [https://www.marketmechina.com/marketing-in-china-how-chinese-audiences-differ-from-western-audiences/] Accessed 17 March 2021.
- *Traction: How Any Startup Can Achieve Explosive Customer Growth*, Justin Mares and Gabriel Weinberg, August 2014.
- *20 Epic Fails in Global Branding*, Geoffrey James, Inc.com, [https://www.inc.com/geoffrey-james/the-20-worst-brand-translations-of-all-time.html] Accessed 4 April 2021.

Chapter 13

- *Expats Looking for a Job in Indonesia*, [https://www.expat.or.id/business/jobseekers.html]
- *Expatriate Workers in Indonesia: New Regulation on Positions Open for Employment*, 13 September, Asean Briefing 2019, [https://www.aseanbriefing.com/news/expatriate-workers-in-indonesia-new-regulation-on-positions-open-for-employment/] accessed 22 March 2021.
- *Guide to Doing Business in Indonesia*, Australia Indonesia Business Council, [https://www.aibc.com.au/pdf/Guide-to-doing-business-in-indonesia.pdf] accessed 22 March 2021.
- *Is there a quota for hiring expats in China?*, Asiapedia, January 2015, [https://www.dezshira.com/library/qa/is-there-quota-for-hiring-expats-in-china-1657.html] accessed 22 March 2021.
- *Export Markets – India*, Austrade, [https://www.austrade.gov.au/australian/export/export-markets/countries/india/doing-business/tariffs-and-regulations] accessed 22 March 2021.
- *Export Markets, United Arab Emirates*, Austrade, [https://www.austrade.gov.au/australian/export/export-markets/countries/united-arab-emirates/doing-business/tariffs-and-regulations] accessed 22 March 2021.
- *Don't say cheese: Amsterdam turns against English usage in shops*, The Guardian Newspaper, 27 January 2018, [https://www.theguardian.com/world/2018/jan/26/dutch-cheese-heads-told-to-close-amsterdam-shop] accessed 5 April 2021.

Chapter 14

- *Protecting Your Intellectual Property Overseas*, Export Finance and Investment Corporation, 2017, [https://www.exportfinance.gov.au/media/4889/efic-protecting-your-ip-overseas-specialist-paper.pdf] Accessed 19 May 2017.
- *A case in point: real-life IPR infringement cases*, Eurobiz Online, 6 December 2016, [https://www.eurobiz.com.cn/case-point-real-life-ipr-infringement-cases/] accessed 5 April 2021.
- *Andō Momofuku: An Inventor Who Used His Noodle to Change Global Food Culture*, Nippon.com, 17 April 2018, [https://www.nippon.com/en/views/b07206/?pnum=2] Accessed 6 April 2021.
- *TIPO guidelines on examining trademark contrary to public order or good morals*, Formosa Transnational Attorneys at Law, 14 October 2015,[https://www.lexology.com/library/detail.aspx?g=bbafc39c-9a4d-466e-9e66-c72888749529] Accessed 6 April 2021.

Chapter 15

- [https://www.healyconsultants.com/uae-company-registration/fees-timelines/] Accessed 29 March 2021.
- *Advancing Trade Development: A Study into International Trade Promotion*, Export Council of Australia, 2015.

Chapter 16

- *5 best practices for hiring the best talent in a global economy*, ADP, [https://www.adp.com/spark/articles/5-best-practices-for-hiring-the-best-talent-in-a-global-economy-9-435.aspx]
- *Recruiting Daily*, [http://recruitingdaily.com/hiring-global-talent/know]
- [http://managing-virtual-teams.com/en/virtual-teams-articles/human-resources/psychological-traits-of-global-workers.html]
- *Recruiting: can everybody work in a global team?*, [https://managing-virtual-teams.com/en/virtual-teams-articles/human-resources/270-global-team-psychological-traits]

About the author

Cynthia Dearin is an international business strategist and lawyer, and the founder of Dearin & Associates.

With 23 years of international experience, she is on a mission to empower business owners and CEOs to scale internationally and amplify their impact in the world.

An Australian-qualified legal practitioner, Cynthia worked in the UK, US, Europe and Middle East, as an Australian diplomat and as a management consultant. She also spent three years as the CEO of the Australia Arab Chamber of Commerce & Industry.

Cynthia is proficient in Arabic and French, both of which she uses professionally. Her first book is *Camels, Sheikhs and Billionaires: Your Guide to Business Culture in the Middle East and North Africa.*

Dearin & Associates

Dearin & Associates helps founders and CEOs to scale their companies internationally and amplify their impact in the world.

We believe that international trade makes the world a better place. We also believe that small companies deserve the opportunity to be internationally successful. Our mission is to create the next generation of international success stories.

Our special focus is to speed up and de-risk the international expansion process for micro-to-medium sized companies and to help them get their products and services to the world.

We provide world-class consultancy services to companies 'go global'. We do this by providing commercial intelligence, creating market entry strategies, supporting companies to execute international strategies to a high standard and introducing the right investors, clients, partners and distributors in international markets.